Cornwall
from the
Coast Path

Michael Kent
& Merryn Kent

Alison Hodge

First published in 2008 by
Alison Hodge, 2 Clarence Place, Penzance,
Cornwall TR18 2QA, UK
www.alison-hodge.co.uk   info@alison-hodge.co.uk

ISBN-13 978-0-906720-68-4

British Library Cataloguing-in-Publication Data
A catalogue record for this book is available from the British
Library.

Designed by Kim Laughton

Originated by BDP –
Book Design and Production, Penzance, Cornwall

Printed in China.

Contents

Introduction

Cornwall's coast is special. Cornish residents, new settlers and visitors alike cherish its spectacular scenery, rich and varied wildlife, history and cultural heritage.

In June 2007, Michael Kent fulfilled a long-standing ambition to walk the whole Cornish Coast Path from Marsland to Cremyll. He took 16 days and walked about 300 miles (approximately 480 km).

During his journey, Mike recorded his thoughts and observations in photographs and notes. On his return, Mike and his wife, Merryn, revisited together some of the places he had passed through.

They investigated further to find out more about the people, landscapes, wildlife and places that had caught Mike's imagination on his walk. Some places, such as the world-famous Tintagel Castle and the tin mines of Levant, were already familiar. Others, like the cliff-side hut built by poet and playwright Ronald Duncan, were new discoveries.

Michael Kent at Bude, at the start of his walk around the Cornish coast.*

The book is divided into 16 chapters – one for each day of the journey. Although not intended as a detailed guide, each chapter includes a map showing the part of the coast covered and some of the places visited. The mileage given in the chapter heading is that along the official South West Coast Path. It does not include diversions, forced and unforced, or wrong turnings.

Mike's account of his journey makes up the main body of the text. The boxes include material uncovered during Merryn and Mike's researches after the journey was completed. Most of the photographs in the book were taken by Mike, using a Pentax Optio W10; being waterproof, lightweight and small, this digital camera was ideal for carrying on a journey where every ounce in the rucksack counted.

Photographs in the main text taken during the walk are identified by an asterisk in the caption. These are not always the best images, but they reflect what was experienced on the particular day a section was walked. Mike's other photographs were taken when places were revisited between July and December 2007, and in February 2008.

The remaining photographs were taken by expert photographers. They were chosen either because they captured a particular scene in a special way, or because they were of something that Mike had not been able to photograph.

When Mike completed his odyssey, he summed up his experiences in one word: 'Fantastic!' We hope this book will help others to share Mike's rediscovery of our own wonderful county, and our passion for Cornwall's rich coastal heritage.

Michael and Merryn Kent
Wadebridge, 2008

Note that the boxed text is colour-coded as follows:

history and archaeology

marine

ornithology

flora

fauna

geology

Day 1 (18.2 ml/29.2 km)

Welcombe to Crackington Haven

Merryn dropped me off at Welcombe village, pointed me towards Marsland and, at precisely 9.22 a.m. on 3 June, I took the first step on my great adventure. For this was to be no Sunday morning stroll, but a walk of about 300 miles (approximately 480 km) around the edge of Cornwall.

After traipsing through a couple of fields, I reached the Coast Path which descends to Marsland Mouth. Towards the top of the path at its steepest part, I found a small hut perched precariously on the cliff. As it was open to passers-by, I went in and was greeted by a dramatic seascape and a wealth of information about the hut's history. I'd only just started, and already I'd stumbled into Ronald Duncan's Hut.

This was a pleasant distraction on the Devon side of the border. Nevertheless, I was delighted when I completed the descent to Marsland Mouth, and crossed the small stream into Cornwall. Home again at last!

I am not one of those people who can make a home wherever they live. As permanent as a marriage made in heaven, for better or worse, Cornwall is and always will be home to me. Whenever I return, even after a short absence, my spirits are lifted.

Ronald Duncan's Hut, at the top of the path that leads down to Marsland from Welcombe, in Devon.

Ronald Duncan's Hut

The hut was originally used by the Admiralty during wartime, but was rebuilt in 1962 as a personal retreat by the poet and playwright Ronald Duncan. For the next 20 years he spent many solitary hours composing poetry as tortuous as the coast on which he looked. The information sheet in the hut describes Duncan as 'highly productive' and, intriguingly, 'notoriously infamous', but does not explain why.

Ronald Duncan (1914–82) is best known for his libretto for Benjamin Britten's opera *The Rape of Lucretia*. His greatest claim to fame in my eyes is that he was scriptwriter for *Girl on a Motorcycle* – a film I much enjoyed when I first saw it at 18. Other works include *Don Juan*; *The Death of Satan: a comedy*, and *The Catalyst: a comedy in two acts*. The latter was probably the work that made him 'notoriously infamous', for it involved a *ménage à trois*, and stirred up controversy when it first appeared in 1957. A third edition of the play is, appropriately enough, published by the Rebel Press of Bideford.

After Duncan's death, the hut fell into disrepair, but it has since been restored by Tim Neville and Briony Lawson, Duncan's daughter. The restoration involved clambering up and down the path to Marsland Mouth more than 100 times to get rid of old stone and acquire new material. This must have been a true labour of love. I only had to make one trip down the steep path, and I didn't fancy making a single return journey. Neville's and Lawson's efforts have not been in vain: the hut has become a welcome shelter for walkers along this barren, windswept stretch of the coast. Above all, the hut is a fitting memorial to a character as untameable as the seas that shaped the magnificent cliffs on which it stands.

*The bridge over the stream that separates Devon from Cornwall at Marsland Mouth.**

Cornwall's shield of arms

The sign marking entry into Cornwall has a rough carving of the county's shield of arms alongside two names: *Cornwall* and *Kernow*. Every Cornish person recognizes the 15 golden balls, or bezants, on the shield as symbolic of Cornwall, but their origin is unknown. Some say they represent the 15 gold coins paid as a ransom for a captured Earl of Cornwall; others claim they represent the months spent by Richard the Lionheart in a German prison after returning from the crusades. All the stories agree that the shield is a crusader's, and that the balls somehow represent the generosity of the Cornish and their willingness to help someone seen as one of their own.

As usual, the border was patrolled by grey clouds threatening rain, but this did not deter me from crossing the small bridge over the stream that separates Devon from Cornwall. Just a metre or so beyond the far end, a wooden sign confirmed that I was back on Cornish soil.

On my way up Marsland Cliff, I was buzzed by a tiger moth. Not the legendary biplane used to train most RAF pilots in the Second World War, but a striking lepidopteran. There are several species of tiger moths. This was the scarlet tiger moth (*Callimorpha dominula*). Resting on the ground with its forewings over its back (top right), it's difficult to understand why this moth with the pronounced ebony and ivory wing pattern acquired the 'scarlet' part of its name. A little further along the path, I came across one unfortunate decapitated individual that looked as if it had crash landed. With its forewings extended (bottom right), the moth revealed bright, orangey-scarlet hind-wings and abdomen.

The scarlet tiger moth (Callimorpha dominula).*

Most day-flying moths are inconspicuous little things. But the scarlet tiger moth does not have to hide itself. During its larval stage it feeds mainly on comfrey (*Symphytum officinale*), a flowering plant common on the cliffs around Marsland. Although comfrey is used as a medicinal herb, its leaves and roots contain small amounts of toxic alkaloids that can cause liver damage if absorbed in large amounts. Scarlet tiger moth larvae extract these chemicals from the comfrey and store them. This makes the moth taste very bitter. It has evolved into a big and flashy insect to warn potential predators that eating it would not be a pleasant experience. Perhaps the individual I found was left lying on the path after a bird spat it out in disgust.

As I continued to the top of Marsland Cliff, a brief seaward glance at the heavily folded strata of Gull Rock reminded me that the North Cornwall coast is as famous for its geology as for its wildlife.

Once I reached the top of Marsland Cliff, I had successfully negotiated my first combe, or steep-sided valley. It was a painful foretaste of what was to come. I had read in *The South West Coast Path Guide* that this is '… probably the most difficult section of the whole Coast Path'. But reading about something and experiencing it are two completely different things. Colin Pringle, a zoologist friend I was to meet later in Marazion, has spent much time in Nepal. He ranks walking the cliffs of the North Coast as being as hard as hiking in the foothills of the Himalayas.

After negotiating two more punishing combes, I caught my first sight of Morwenstow valley, famous as the home of one the great characters of North Cornwall, the Revd R.S. Hawker. When Hawker was offered a living at Morwenstow in 1834, he jumped at the chance of going back to the

The heavily folded strata of Gull Rock.

area he had loved as a child. He treasured this remote place within sight and sound of the sea, and was to remain the vicar there until his death in 1875.

The vicarage at Morwenstow

During his time at Morwenstow, Hawker restored the Norman church dedicated to St Morwenna and St John the Baptist, and built a new vicarage close by. The vicarage is dominated by its large, tower-like chimneys. Some are based on the towers of churches in Hawker's life, such as those at Welcombe and at Magdalen, his old college at Oxford. The

kitchen chimney, however, is a replica of his mother's tomb. This is just one example of Hawker's many eccentricities. He was also to be found dressing up as a mermaid and sitting on rocks close to the sea talking to birds, and taking services in brightly coloured clothes rather than the usual drab black or grey vestments. My favourite foible is that after inviting his cats into church for services, Hawker 'excommunicated' one for catching mice on Sundays.

The turf-covered roof of Hawker's Hut, looking towards Sharpnose Point.

Before coming to Morwenstow, Hawker had gained fame as the writer of *The Song of the Western Men*, more commonly known in Cornwall as *Trelawney*. As I walked along the valley, I blared out my own rendition of this song which has become the Cornish National Anthem. When sung by thousands at a county rugby match, the sound is spine-tingling. I don't doubt that my solo rendition would have been just as positively received, but unfortunately there was absolutely no one within earshot to appreciate it.

As well as a remarkable vicarage, Hawker also built a hut much smaller than Duncan's, but just as interesting, on top of Vicarage Cliff. Made of driftwood with a turf-covered roof, Hawker's Hut, as it is now known, is the smallest and probably the humblest property under the care of the National Trust. I went inside and sat there for a while but, unlike Hawker, I wrote no poetry (not even by contributing to the verses carved on the wooden benches). Nor, I hasten to add, did I partake of an opium pipe as was Hawker's custom. But, as Hawker himself must have done thousands of times, I did look along the beach and out towards the Point and the sea beyond.

It was a relatively tranquil scene, but it was easy to imagine how dangerous and frightening the high waves of a ferocious storm could be in this area. One particularly infamous storm occurred on 8 September 1842 when the *Caledonian*, a Scottish brig of about 450 tonnes (500 tons), came to a sad end on the rocks of Sharpnose Point.

Hawker and the *Caledonian*

The *Caledonian* was on its way from Falmouth to Gloucester. A fierce north-westerly gale was pressing the ship closer and closer to the shore. At about 1 p.m., despite the efforts of its captain, Peter Stevenson, huge waves smashed the ship against the rocks. The mast crashed to the deck, throwing everyone into the sea.

Controversy surrounds the incident. It has been rumoured that the ship was enticed on to the rocks by wreckers, and even that Hawker was involved in this skulduggery. According to his biographer, Sabine Baring-Gould, Hawker did everything he could to help the wrecked sailors, despite the reluctance of others. His claret coat protecting him from the wind, he hurried down to the beach as fast as he could to help organize a rescue. Although he found the lifeboat men already on the beach, their vessel had not been launched. To his disgust, the men had listened to the entreaties of their wives not to take one step until the *Caledonian* was completely abandoned and legally available for salvage. Hawker pleaded with the lifeboat men to help save the distressed sailors, but his appeals fell on deaf ears. In the words of Sabine Baring-Gould, 'Above the clamour of their shrill voices, and the sough of the wind, rose the roar of the vicar's voice; he was convulsed with indignation, and poured forth the most sacred appeals to their compassion for drowning sailors.'

With no other signs of help, Hawker went to fetch the lifeboat himself, but it was too late. All but one of the ten-man crew of the *Caledonian* died. Their bodies were carried up the steep cliff to be buried in the churchyard, where a white figurehead of the *Caledonian* was erected in memory of her captain and crew. The survivor, Edward La Daine from Jersey, was found by a farmer and under Hawker's orders was taken to the vicarage. Here La Daine was nursed until he recovered from his ordeal.

In all, Revd Hawker buried over 40 sailors who were drowned at sea and washed up at the bottom of Vicarage Cliff. At a time when it was general practice to dump drowned sailors unceremoniously in unmarked graves on the beach or cliffs, or even to let them rot in the water, Hawker demonstrated great compassion by making sure every one of the drowned bodies had a full Christian burial.

From Hawker's Hut, I continued up Vicarage Cliff and past Higher Sharpnose Point. The path that leads to the end of the Point passes along the top of a splendid ridge spur. It slopes down steeply on both sides, making it a dangerous place for the unwary. I knew from horror stories of people falling off Striding Edge in the Lake District that walking along such ridges was dangerous in high winds. With a blustery breeze blowing, I decided against taking any unnecessary risks, and was satisfied with a look at the ridge from a safe distance. Then I pressed on towards Cleave, where I was confronted by the giant satellite-tracking dishes on the former RAF station. The first hint of their rather spooky presence was on the skyline above Morwenstow. As I drew closer to what is now called Government Communications Headquarters (GCHQ) Bude, they came increasingly to dominate my view and thoughts. I could not help but wonder what really goes on there. The signs warning against trespassing on Government property, the ring of double-fencing, and the close-circuit television cameras were enough to tell me that casual enquiries or an informal poke-around would not be welcome.

As fascinating as GCHQ Bude is, I felt relieved to put its intimidating presence behind me and continue my journey westwards. I paused at

GCHQ, Bude
Not surprisingly, the activities at such British intelligence stations usually remain highly classified. However, when some European Union (EU) member states expressed concern that the station was involved in industrial espionage and the tapping of civilian communications, a few details about its activities were made public. According to a report made in 2001 by the European Parliament, there are 21 dishes in all, three wider than 30 metres in diameter. Each is positioned and orientated towards the satellites of the INTELSAT, INTERSPUTNIK and INMARSAT networks that transmit over much of the Northern hemisphere from the Atlantic Ocean to the Indian Ocean. The purpose of the dishes is to gather information that might be useful to the British Intelligence Service. According to its own website:

> GCHQ has two missions: signals intelligence (Sigint) and Information Assurance. Our Sigint work protects the vital interests of the nation: we provide information to support Government decision making in the fields of national security, military operations and law enforcement. The intelligence we provide is at the heart of the struggle against terrorism and also contributes to the prevention of serious crime.

Steeple Point to take a drink of water and admire the view. A low spring tide had exposed the extensive wave-cut platforms, intertidal reefs and sea-borne sandbanks that make up much of the shoreline between Duckpool and Bude. Despite the drizzle, the scene was so breathtaking that my mind turned almost immediately from thoughts of espionage and intrigue to matters marine biological. The rocky shores are not just mineral products of the area's geological past. Much of their surface is covered with living organisms – common seaweeds, mussels, limpets, barnacles, and the not-so-common marine bristle worm, or honeycomb worm (*Sabellaria alveolata*, page 14).

At Duckpool, I examined the reefs of honeycomb worms, then made my way to Sandymouth where I joined Merryn for lunch at the National Trust café. Refuelled and well watered, we walked above the stretches of golden sand along the Coast Path to Bude. An interesting feature of the town is the canal, constructed in the 1820s to carry calcium-rich sea-sand from the beaches of Bude Bay to farms up to 35 miles (56 km) inland. The lock at the seaward end of the canal was opened in 1823 to allow

The extensive wave-cut platforms between Duckpool and Bude.*

 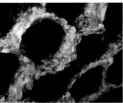 

Honeycomb worm (*Sabellaria alveolata*)

Groups of this gregarious, segmented worm live in tightly packed tubes that commonly form hummocks (left) more than 1 metre (3 ft) across and 50 cm (20 in) thick. The worms (right) cannot leave their tubes (middle), but when the tide is in, they extend their heads and long tentacles out into the sea to capture passing plankton to eat and collect sand grains to extend their tubes. The appearance of clusters of hexagonal-shaped tubes has earned this reef-builder the common name of honeycomb worm.

The honeycomb worm is fussy about where it lives. It occurs only where the seawater is clean and well oxygenated; where wave action is strong enough to stir up fresh supplies of food and building material, but not so strong that it might wash away the tubes; and where there is a plentiful supply of exactly the right type of sand to make its home. Only the purest coarse sand, rich in shell fragments is good enough. This is exactly what is freely available on the shores between Duckpool and Widemouth. The high shell content also made the sand so valuable to farmers that in the 1820s a canal was built to transport it from Bude to farms inland.

coastal merchant ships to gain access to the wharfs in Bude. The nearby breakwater was built to protect the lock entrance from the full force of the open sea.

When I could delay my departure no longer, I turned towards the Coast Path, lifted my fully laden rucksack on to my back and said goodbye to Merryn. She drove off, abandoning me to my fate. With my temporary accommodation and all essential equipment strapped securely behind me, I proceeded, plodding like a very overweight tortoise, past the tower at Compass Point and towards Widemouth Bay.

The Temple of Winds
The octagonal-sided tower at Compass Point was built of local sandstone by Thomas Acland in 1840. He called it The Temple of Winds after the Athenian building which has a similar design, but many locals prefer to call it The Pepper Pot, or simply The Compass Tower, because of the compass points cut into the sides. When cliff erosion threatened to destroy the tower, it was moved from its original location to where it is today. According to one source, the result of relocation was that the tower's compass points are about eight degrees out of true alignment. If you have a compass handy, you can check this for yourself. Whatever the accuracy of its bearings, the tower is a magnificent structure from which to view spectacular scenery in all directions.

Between Bude and Widemouth, the Coast Path is so close to the cliff edge that I could hear each individual wave crashing on to the shore below. The sound was made more threatening as I passed by the massive slumps that occur on this actively eroding stretch of cliffs.

About a mile or so from Widemouth, I paused on the high cliffs at Phillip's Point, one of Cornwall Wildlife Trust's smallest reserves. Around the notice-board were flowers you might expect to find there, including whites sea campions, and pinks, or thrift. The notice-board suggested that, by looking out to sea, I might be lucky enough to observe a variety of exciting marine creatures from seals and groups of bottlenose dolphins to basking sharks and even leatherneck turtles. Try as I might I could see nothing. Nevertheless, I enjoyed the spectacular views to Hartland Point, and consoled myself with the thought that there was every chance of seeing some of these creatures over the next couple of weeks.

Beyond Widemouth, the cliffs are so badly eroded that the Coast Path has been diverted along the road – an early reminder that the route of the Cornish Coast Path is continually revised.

Ancient woodland on Dizzard Point.*

Descending yet another steep-sided valley, I reached Millook Haven with its half dozen or so houses and pebble beach, and took a short rest. It's hard to believe that geologists from all over the world come to this quiet cove to see its remarkable rocks. With only time enough for a cursory inspection of the famous zig-zag contortions of grey slate, I took several deep breaths and climbed up to Dizzard Point.

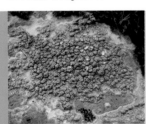

Lichens on the Dizzard

As well as dwarf oaks, the dense Dizzard woods are exceptionally rich in lichens. According to one scientific report, over 130 species have been recorded, and many are rare. Lichens come in three main body forms: crustose (left), foliose (middle), and fructicose (right). All three types are found on the Dizzard.

Each lichen species results from a union between a particular combination of fungus and alga. The fungus provides some protection and essential nutrients to the alga in exchange for photosynthesized food.

Lichens are slow-growing organisms, sensitive to air pollution and habitat disturbance. Some thrive only in ultra-clean ancient woodland such as that on the Dizzard. Ancient woodland is defined as land that has been continuously wooded since AD 1600. It is probable that woods on the Dizzard have always been woodland, back to the pre-Neolithic wildwood.

Dwarf oak in ancient woodland on the Dizzard.

The Dizzard is one of the few places to have ancient woodland dominated by dwarf oak. I had seen these diminutive trees at Piles Copse and Wistman's Wood on Dartmoor, but never in so great a profusion as on the Dizzard. The canopy extends from the top of the cliff down hundreds of metres towards the sea. Trees near the summit, being protected to some extent by those below, grow up to four or five metres tall. But strong south-westerly winds clip the oak close to the cliff edge so savagely that few are more than a metre or so high.

On leaving the Dizzard, I made my way quickly around Pencannow Point, with St Gwennys church in the distance, and descended along the winding path down to Crackington Haven. Even though I took care to keep to the path, and avoided the slippery slabs of slate that led to precipitous cliff tops, I arrived at the Combe Barton Inn well before closing time.

Once inside the warmth and comfort of the hostelry, I was able to shed my load, relax and reflect on the first day of my journey, while sampling the local brew. The wild coastal scenery, fascinating cultural hot-spots, and demanding physical challenge had more than lived up to my expectations. But I was also foot-sore and extremely tired, so I was relieved that I could camp nearby, snuggle into my down-filled sleeping bag, and fall quickly into a sleep so deep that even late-night revellers did not wake me.

Day 2 (16 ml/25.7 km)

Crackington Haven to Tregonnick Tail

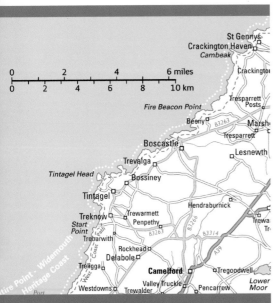

I woke fully rejuvenated just before 6 a.m. Muscles and joints which had been sore, stiff and painful only a few hours before were moving freely again after the miracle of sleep. The soft grass had been as comfortable as any mattress.

I was able to make a quick visit to a convenient convenience nearby before setting up the Trangia to boil water. A Trangia is a very clever device for cooking when you are camping, combining a portable stove with various bits of cooking equipment, such as a kettle and saucepan. The whole thing is lightweight and packs away neatly – ideal for a person walking the Coast Path who doesn't know exactly where he or she is to spend the night.

My first breakfast on the Coast Path consisted of one of my precious saffron buns, helped down with a mug of steaming tea. My energy reserves, diminished after walking up and down countless combes, had been further depleted to make repairs to my body during the night. As simple as my breakfast was, it was a delicious way of refuelling.

While savouring my feast, I recalled that saffron buns and cakes are now a Cornish speciality. Saffron was (and still is) very expensive, and at one time it was a baking ingredient used only for special occasions. Today, every self-respecting Cornish baker supplies saffron buns.

Now ready for the day ahead, I quickly packed away my temporary home, delighted that the silky material of my new tent slipped smoothly into its stuff bag. By 7.30 a.m. I had left my overnight pitch to have a quick look at Crackington Haven's famous rock formations. Then I headed slowly towards Boscastle.

The magnificent sea cliffs at Crackington Haven.

The sky was grey, with a thick mist rolling in from the north and across the valley at Crackington Haven. This made the vegetation so wet that, as I brushed against it, water dripped down my legs and into my boots. The constant sound of the sea splashing against rocks was soon accompanied by the repetitive squelch of each footstep.

When I had to cross a couple of stream-fed marshy valleys, I was relieved to find the areas well managed by the National Trust. The wardens and their co-workers had done such a great job of constructing steps down steep valley sides, and building board-walks across the marsh, that walking was relatively easy, despite my soaking socks.

Although Cambeak looked inviting and solid, several signs warn that the cliffs are dangerously unstable. Graphic signs depicting a man falling over a cliff were reminders of the potentially fatal consequences of ignoring warnings to 'Keep away from the edge'. With my imagination in overdrive, I decided not to scramble along the sharp ridge to the tip of Cam-

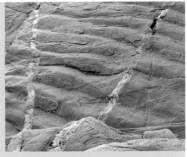

Crackington Haven: geologist's paradise

The excellent North Cornwall District Council information boards proclaim that 'Crackington Haven is a treasure trove for anyone interested in geology.' On the exposed seaward surface of the magnificent sea cliffs, layers of fine-grained dark grey sedimentary rock, estimated to be more than 300 million years old, are evidence that the area was once deep under the surface of a great sea, known as the Rheic Ocean.

The rippled surface seen on parts of the rocky shore are fossilized impressions of the action of the prehistoric ocean on the sea bed. The pale layers sandwiched between the grey sediments in the cliffs are believed to be sandstone that came down from deltas to the north in enormous landslides during periods of cataclysmic disturbances. These powerful quakes were the result of a collision between two great land masses that pushed Cornwall out of the sea. The force of the collision caused some rocks to fold and others to crack under the strain, creating the dramatic geological landscape that we see today.

High Cliff and the John Weaver seat in thick mist, and Northern Door Arch.

beak. Instead, I continued along the main Coast Path above the Northern Door Arch, Samphire Rock and the Strangles beach, towards High Cliff and the John Weaver seat.

At well over 223 metres (730 feet), the summit of High Cliff is the highest point on the Cornish Coast Path. According to guidebooks, on a clear day it provides fantastic views of Lundy Island and South Wales. But Monday 4 June was not such a day. Even the seat was barely visible through the mist that made sea and sky almost indistinguishable.

With no excuse for delay, I turned towards Boscastle, and continued my journey. In the worsening weather, I made a wrong turn and found myself on a minor road. Rather than simply retracing my steps a couple of hundred metres, I decided to continue along the road until I found an alternative route back to the Coast Path. This was not one of my brightest decisions, as it took over an hour to get back to the Coast Path. Eventually I found myself near Pentargon, having unintentionally by-passed Rusey Cliff. It requires a special kind of skill to get lost on the Cornish Coast Path, and I have that skill in abundance.

*The harbour at Boscastle.**

Pentargon is noted for its waterfall. In *The Cornish Coast and Moors* (1912) Folliott-Stokes rated it '… the finest coast fall in Cornwall. The water falls for about eighty feet [24 metres]; then it strikes a shelving ledge, and reaches the shore in a cloud of spray in which the setting sun is weaving little rainbows.' He claimed that it was possible '… to stand between the cliff and this shower of falling water and look out through a veil of prismatic colours at the sea beyond.' But that was almost 100 years ago. Since then cliff falls have caused the old view point on the north side to be lost. As advised by today's guidebooks, I viewed the falls from the safety of the cliff slope below the Coast Path on the south side of Pentargon. In the words of *The South West Coast Path Guide*, 'It's a long way down'!

I reached Boscastle harbour at 11.20 a.m. Approaching it from the Penally Point, I could see why this snaking natural inlet was such an important harbour. But although it is protected from all but the worst seas, its position below the rivers Valency and Jordan make the village vulnerable to flooding.

Few people in Britain can be unaware of the floods that caused such devastation to the harbour and village of Boscastle on 16 August 2004. Though the village has suffered regular flooding for hundreds of years, this was the most devastating on record. The rivers rose frighteningly quickly, and produced a torrent that flooded homes and washed away 80 cars. Amazingly, no lives were lost, thanks to the quick action of the emergency services and local people. The full story of the flood, including television news footage, can be seen in the Visitor Centre – a converted pilchard house on the harbour.

Boscastle: the prettiest harbour in England?

Although the area has been inhabited for a much longer period, Boscastle as a settlement dates from medieval times. The entrance to the harbour snakes inland from the open sea. By the mid-sixteenth century the difficult entry and poor state of repair of the quay made Boscastle a far-from-safe haven. But in 1584 the Sheriff of Cornwall, famous seaman Sir Richard Grenville, gave orders that the quay should be repaired. From this time, Boscastle's harbour grew in importance, until the arrival of the railway in North Cornwall in 1893 led to its decline as an industrial port, and the gradual growth of Boscastle as a tourist centre.

Guidebooks and owners of bed-and-breakfast properties in the area often describe Boscastle as picturesque. Presumably this is meant in the modern sense. The guidebooks are implying that Boscastle is pretty and charming in a rather quaint, old-fashioned way – and so it is. It is worth remembering, however, that 150 years ago the village was a hive of activity and back-breaking work. In the nineteenth century, when the port was at its busiest, you could have seen wagons and carts loading and unloading everything from wines and spirits to slate and china clay. The port boasted a forge, a boatyard and a limekiln. There were alehouses and warehouses. The whole place would have been bustling with people, horses and traffic. Not the kind of place most modern visitors to Cornwall look for in a holiday destination. But even in the nineteenth century the area had its admirers, the most famous being Thomas Hardy who came with his new wife, Emma.

Early visitors to Boscastle appreciated what the modern tourist, attracted by the pretty cottages, the delightful harbour and the gift shops, is in danger of missing. The village is more than a charming distraction. It is sheltered by magnificent cliffs that give the place a disturbing, rather claustrophobic feel. Far from lessening Boscastle's attractions, this adds to the grandeur and beauty of the village and its unspoilt, coastal setting. Boscastle is picturesque in the original sense of the word, combining the natural and man-made to create a varied, wild landscape that is pleasing to the eye.

As I walked along the harbour and through the village, I was greatly impressed by the recovery made and the work that is still in progress to defend the village from further severe flooding. Channels were being cleared and deepened, and new bridges constructed to conserve what many regard as the prettiest harbour in England.

From Boscastle, I grunted my way like a tennis player up the steep path to Willapark, where I paused briefly to take a look at the distinctive whitewashed tower on the cliff top.

According to information in the Visitor Centre, the tower at Willapark was originally built in the 1820s as a 'pleasure house' for a Thomas Avery. A local merchant with the reputation of a hard and ruthless man, Avery was described by contemporaries as 'a notorious wrecker and receiver of contraband'. On one occasion he was found guilty of attempting to rob Preventive Men (customs officers of the day) of a cargo of hops they had taken in custody from a wreck. It is ironic that his tower is now used by coastguards to protect ships and their cargo.

From the Coastguard station at Willapark, I skirted the ancient strip fields of Forrabury Common and the slate quarries of Western Blackapit; negotiated the steep valley at Welltown Farm, and headed towards Rocky Valley. With the humidity high and a grey sky threatening heavy rain, the

Looking towards the tower at Willapark.

Puffins and other auks

The stretch of coast between Tintagel and Boscastle is probably one of the best places in Cornwall to see puffins (*Fratercula arctica*), guillemots (*Uria aalge*) and razorbills (*Alca torda*) – all members of the auk family. During the breeding season, these oceanic birds come to North Cornwall to breed on our cliffs and islands, and to feed in our inshore waters.

A puffin, with its squat body shape, smart plumage and colourful bill is easily distinguished from the other two which, at a distance, are easily confused. At close range the two larger auks can be distinguished by their beaks and coloration. A razorbill has a rectangular bill, no furrow behind its eyes, and lack of a prominent dark half-collar on its neck. A guillemot has a long, pointed bill; sharp, dark furrow behind its eyes, and a U-shaped throat pattern.

One of the most fascinating features of the puffin is its uncanny ability to catch and carry several fish at once. Puffins seem to be particularly fond of sand eels. Those intended for the young are stacked crosswise in a parent's bill, usually up to a dozen or so at a time. One particularly adept bird is recorded as carrying an amazing total of 62 fish in its beak: 61 sand-eels and one three-bearded rockling.

conditions were far from perfect for photography or bird watching. As I walked past Ladies Window, a great place to view the auks on Short and Long islands (home to the largest puffin colony in Cornwall), I vowed to return with local photographer Adrian Langdon on a better day.

Looking out from Ladies Window – a great place to view auks on Short and Long Islands.

The waterfall in Rocky Valley.

With its gorge cut deep into the cliff, and running spectacularly down to the sea, you can see immediately why this is *the* Rocky Valley of the North Cornwall coast. Although Merryn and I have visited it often, this valley never fails to enchant us with its beauty and mystery.

Leaving the valley, I climbed the steps to the path that skirts Bossinney cove. Plodding past this secluded spot, I found it hard to believe that Bossinney once had its own Member of Parliament.

Just beyond Bossiney, I approached Tintagel Haven, and reached the foot of the legendary Castle. Pausing to take a good look at its outstandingly beautiful site but less-than-beautiful remains, I wondered if the Castle would have become such a popular tourist attraction without its Arthurian connection.

The enchantment and mystery of Rocky Valley

Between Boscastle and Bossiney Cove, Rocky Valley is well worth a diversion. From the Coast Path, the valley begins as a narrow, rocky gorge where a small river tumbles into the sea. When the tide is high and the wind is up, the rocks around the entrance are dangerous, and a sign warns people away: you could easily be swept into the deep gulley below. But the walk up the valley is both safe and impressive, the steep sides of the gorge giving way to a gentler wooded landscape.

It isn't far to the deserted mill, which produced cloth in the eighteenth and nineteenth centuries. Of particular interest here are the maze patterns carved into the smooth, shale rock-face. A plaque confidently pronounces them to be Bronze Age, but they are likely to be much more recent than this, probably no more than 250 years old. Not that this makes the labyrinths any less interesting. They might well have been carved by one of the mill tenants as a kind of personal mark. As this person was probably not classically educated, it seems surprising that the carver knew this type of pattern well enough to reproduce it. Recent scholarship suggests there was a widespread folk knowledge of this kind of maze pattern in the late eighteenth and early nineteenth centuries.

Whatever the source of the maze carvings, over the years people have wanted to leave their own personal mark. Even as a child in the 1960s, Merryn has dim memories of seeing rags and handkerchiefs left as tokens (or prayer offerings) on branches. Although there are still a few handkerchiefs, modern offerings include everything from wind chimes to hair bands. More destructively, some people have taken to hammering coins into the rocks around the carvings, with the danger that the rocks may eventually split, and the intriguing carvings be lost for ever.

From Tintagel Haven, I walked through the National Trust property at Glebe cliff, past the Youth Hostel and the extensive rock outcrops favoured by sea anglers, on to the disused slate quarries between Tregatta and Trebarwith. The path goes scarily close to cliff-face quarries that plummet straight down 24 metres (80 feet) or so. It beggars belief how men could actually do hard manual work in such a dangerous location.

Soon after safely negotiating the quarries, I reached Trebarwith Strand. Tired after being on the path for more than 12 hours, I was keen to reach the campsite next to the Port William Hotel, my planned place of rest. Unfortunately, I had based my plan on Mason's *Walk the Cornish Coastal Path*, which was published in 1995. Since then, inconsiderately, the cliff-edge site has fallen into the sea.

After a thirst-quenching shandy, I resorted to plan B: finding some bed and breakfast accommodation in Trebarwith Village. This plan was also doomed to fail: no one seems to offer B&B in the village any more. As a final resort, I decided to camp wild on the cliffs of the Tregonnick trail, a

The road down to Tintagel Haven from Tintagel village.

Tintagel Castle

The village and castle at Tintagel are inseparable from the legend of King Arthur. The blame for this can be laid at the door of a man called Geoffrey of Monmouth. About 800 years ago, he suggested Tintagel as the place where Arthur was conceived. From this tenuous link, it was a short step to thinking of Tintagel as the place where Arthur grew up. People then began to believe that King Arthur reigned from Tintagel and so, despite the lack of any evidence, the castle became Camelot. It has to be said that the tourist industry which has grown up as a result has done little to dispel the idea.

Romantic as is the idea of knights, the round table, and the grail, the truth is that the origins of the castle are shrouded in mystery. Extensive and meticulous excavations have raised lots of possibilities, but few definite answers. From glass, ceramics and coins found in the area, there certainly seems to have been some activity on the site in the late Roman period. Arthur-watchers will be pleased to learn that building work was carried out in the so-called Dark Ages. There also seems to have been extensive trade with the Mediterranean and North Africa. It is likely that Tintagel supported a thriving and important community at this time, even if it was not the legendary castle of heroic knights.

The castle at Tintagel whose remains are seen by modern visitors was built by Earl Richard of Cornwall in the thirteenth century. On the face of it, Tintagel is one of the least sensible places in Cornwall to build a castle. It is too remote and too low lying to intimidate the locals. The ideal place for a castle is on the top of a hill, where it serves as a constant reminder to the peasantry, every time they raise their eyes, of its owner's strength and authority. From a hilltop, the castle owner can easily survey the surrounding countryside, and keep a watch for attackers. Tintagel Castle is not in an ideal defensive position either. The eminent Cornish historian Charles Thomas said that it was 'more fittingly described as a folly.' It is more than likely that Earl Richard knew that Tintagel had symbolic importance in the eyes of the Cornish, and wanted to claim some of that symbolic authority for himself.

The Pinnacle at Lanterdan

High-quality Upper Devonian slate has been extracted from the cliffs around Trebarwith since the fifteenth century. The best and largest slabs were 'exported', but much of the slate was used locally and can still be seen in stiles made shiny from the impact of quarrymen's boots; the herringbone, or 'curzy-way', stone hedges, and the fence posts. At one time, as many as ten quarries were worked in the area. Lanterdan quarry, in which the 24-metre (80-foot) high pinnacle stands, was of the common hole-in-the ground type, from which enormous volumes of slate were extracted. According to a National Trust information leaflet, the pinnacle might have avoided demolition by the quarrymen's hammer and drill simply because it had no slate worth working. Another possibility is that the pinnacle was retained as a 'poppet head' – a structure from which a cableway was stretched to an anchorage point on the opposite cliff. This allowed slate to be carried from one part of the quarry to another. Whatever the reason for its existence, this man-made tower is a magnificent relic of quarrying days.

couple of miles south of Trebarwith Strand. Fortunately, I found a sheltered site on a grassy ledge overlooking the sea.

After the day's rather miserable weather, it was a glorious evening with the setting sun reflecting mirage-like images off the sea. I made camp, ate a hearty hot meal; vowed to make future plans using up-to-date information, and fell once again into a deep sleep.

Day 3 (15.7 ml/25.2 km)

Tregonnick Tail to Padstow

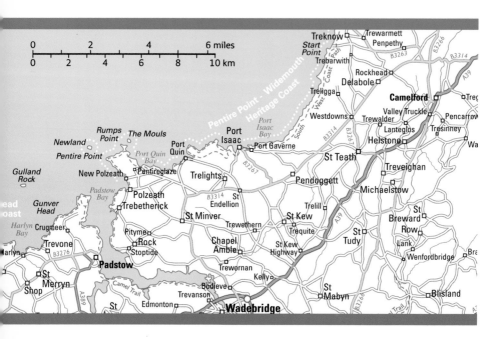

I woke to the sound of waves lapping against rocks as the tide was coming in just below my pitch. The wave-cut rocky platform and sandy shore which make up the beach are only accessible during the few hours of low tide. With no possibility of enjoying a seashore safari, I made a simple breakfast and prepared to depart.

With the last of my water gone in an early morning brew, I felt thirsty even before I departed. I had not planned to camp wild at Tregonnick Tail and had brought only a single flask full of water down to this secluded spot. The previous day's hard walking had left me partially dehydrated, and I was keen to get a refill.

I quickly set off towards Port Gaverne, where I was confident I could obtain fresh supplies. But even before I reached Delabole Point and the spectacular Barrett's Zawn (a tunnel down which slate was once hauled),

*A pool of fresh water in a stream beside the Coast Path,
on the way to Port Gaverne.*

my mind was dominated by thoughts of water. I knew that to keep in best condition, walkers should drink about three to five litres of water per day. As thirst is a poor indicator of the body's need, it's best to take a drink every hour at least, even if you do not feel like it. I also recalled that not needing to urinate as much as normal, and producing a dark urine are signs of dehydration. There was no doubt in my mind that I was in danger of becoming seriously dehyrdrated and needed water soon.

Like the ancient mariner in Coleridge's poem, I had 'water, water everywhere nor any drop to drink'. Not only was there seawater to the right of me in the vastness of the ocean, but there was also fresh water to the left of me, trickling down the streams and dropping over the cliffs. The sea with its dehyrdating salt might just as well have been desert, but the stream water looked clear and tantalizingly thirst-quenching. Mindful that streams will have passed through farmland and by roads, picking up pesticides and other pollutants on the way, for a while I resisted the temptation to draw water from them. But as the sun came out to tease me and the going got tougher, I succumbed. Choosing a stream with clear water running through and no farm or roads within sight, I filled a kettle of water. Still wary, I boiled the water for more than the mandatory five minutes to get rid of any parasites, and hoped that the freshwater plants and bacteria further up the stream had done their purification job, just as they do in sewage treatment plants.

*The little cove of Port Gaverne.**

I had a mug of tea, put the remaining water in my flask, and let it cool in the flowing stream. It was amazing how deliciously refreshing that water tasted to my parched mouth. I vowed not to take this simple pleasure for granted when I returned home and a tap was no more than a few paces away.

I approached Port Gaverne by the Great Slate Road down to the beach. Quarried out in 1807, the Road enabled carts to carry Delabole slate down to Port Gaverne. From there, it was loaded on to vessels going to and from Barnstaple, Bristol and beyond. Due to the narrowness of the harbour, the larger boats were unable to turn around. They had to be pulled back out to sea using a system of ropes and chains that passed through metal hoops secured into rocks outside the harbour. When the North Cornwall Railway Company linked Delabole to Launceston and Plymouth, the slate trade stopped. But the railway provided a speedy means of transporting pilchard from the village to large ports from which it could be exported to Italy and the West Indies.

Although I had taken the Great Slate Road, there is an alternative route into Port Gaverne through an area known as The Main. This is a longer, more scenic and interesting route. It leads from the headland, across a chasm spanned by a well-constructed bridge, along the eastern edge of the harbour to the back of the beach.

The Main has been managed by a local group, The Friends of The Main, since 2002. When I talked to its Chairman, Colin Butler, he described

Pilchards and Port Gaverne

Shoals of pilchards were vital to the economy of many Cornish coves and harbours from the sixteenth century until end of the nineteenth century. *Sardinus pilchardus*, to give it its scientific name, is closely related to the herring. Only adult fish are called pilchards. Those less than one year old are called sardines. Pilchards grow up to 30 centimetres (1 foot) in length, and are generally found in European seas such as the English Channel and the Mediterranean, spending much of their lives in shoals at depths of 60 metres (200 feet) or more.

In most years from the sixteenth century to the beginning of the twentieth century, pilchards came in vast shoals to our shores to feed on plankton between July and September. Each fishing community employed a 'huer' to spot the dark, purple shadows of oncoming shoals, and to direct the fishing boats making the catch. Usually, three boats working together would encircle the shoal with huge seine nets. Wherever possible, the nets would be anchored to the shore. Then, using smaller boats over several days, the pilchards would be lifted from the heaving mass of enclosed fish.

After removal, the pilchards were carried to fish cellars (sometimes called fish palaces) to be preserved. There were two fish cellars in Port Gaverne, both of which are now owned by the National Trust. They consisted of large, rectangular buildings (the cellars) around an open court. In the cellars, the pilchards were placed in salt-covered layers for about four weeks. French sea salt was generally preferred because of its high quality. After preservation, the fish would be washed and stacked tight in straight-sided barrels by pressing them down with weights.

Oil emanating from the pressed fish was a valuable by-product used, among other things, as a fuel for lighting lamps in London. Often, the money obtained from the oil was sufficient to cover all the costs of fish production, leaving the revenue from the preserved fish as a clear profit.

Most pilchards went to Italy to satisfy the demand for fish during periods of abstention from meat-eating among the Catholic population. Some went to the West Indian sugar plantations to feed slaves.

The pilchard industry declined in the mid-twentieth century with changes in the migratory movements of the fish. They are still caught off Cornwall, but in much smaller quantities than in times past.

some of the group's activities: the back-breaking, thorn-pricking scrub clearance that encourages a wealth of flowers, insects, and birds to the area, and the construction work, essential for maintaining public access into and out of the area. It was the Friends who, at a fraction of the cost of professional builders, got together to build the bridge along which I walked. Talking to Colin, it was clear that though the work has been hard at times, it has been well worth it. Not only has it helped to conserve the environment, but by bringing locals together to share the challenges, it has also helped to generate a great community spirit.

Looking towards Port Isaac. *

Walking westwards from Port Gaverne, I followed the pavement and reached a garage on the road above Port Isaac. While drivers refilled their vehicles with fossil fuel, I rehydrated my body with 'clear, cool water from Cornish springs'. After imitating a camel at an oasis, I made my way down into the harbour village, known to many through the Doctor Martin television series as Port Wenn.

Having bought my first pasty of the trip, and a one-and-a-half litre bottle of water (I was still thirsty!), I sat on the slipway and considered how much this fishing village has changed since it was first established as a port in medieval times. Those who laboured during Port Isaac's industrious, smelly and dirty past would no doubt suffer an initial shock at today's tourist-driven quaintness. But if the atmosphere has changed, a lot of the town would be familiar. Much of the Platt (the local name for the harbour area); the remains of the pier, which dates back to the reign of Henry VIII, and the 'opes' (the narrow streets that wind their way around the harbour), such as the aptly named Squeeze-Belly-Alley, have changed little since the 1500s.

Leaving Port Isaac past the Wesleyan Chapel up Roscarrock Hill, I soon reached the cliff-top fields, with splendid views back to the harbour. After descending into Pinehaven, I braced myself for the stiff climb up the steps towards Varley Head. I started to count the steps and, sweat-

Kellan Head, looking back towards Tintagel. *

ing buckets, got to 150 when a jogger whizzed past. With his bronzed, weather-beaten face and silvery hair glistening in the sun, and his deck shoes and blue-and-white-striped T-shirt, he looked like an old but very fit seaman. Surprised and distracted from my exertions, I thought that he might be a ghost of one of the many who smuggled (or, as he would have preferred to call it, 'free-traded') along the coast of Cornwall. Perhaps, I speculated, he was doomed to run the Coast Path forever in an eternal bid to escape the clutches of the Preventive Water Guard, or HM Coast-guard as it later became. Clearly becoming delusional from dehydration, I stopped and took a swig of water before continuing. With my thoughts still on the smuggler careering off into the distance, I forgot to restart counting the steps and still do not know how many there are to the top of the cliffs.

From Varley Head to Kellan Head, a party of children played 'hare and tortoise' with me, dashing ahead one minute and stopping the next, allowing me to overtake and be overtaken at least half a dozen times. After reaching Kellan Head they returned towards Port Isaac, while I paused to look back towards Tintagel. It was very satisfying to see just how far I had travelled in the last couple of days.

Following the path on its switchback course around Kellan Head, I arrived at Port Quin.

Back on the Coast Path, I went out to Doyden Point and its folly. The headland was bought in 1827 by Samuel Symons, who subsequently built the curious castellated structure with its short, gothic tower in which to entertain friends. Symons, a wealthy Wadebridge man, had a reputation for living the good life, and the folly became a venue for many lively drinking and gambling parties. Now a National Trust cottage, it has the more genteel purpose of providing a secluded holiday retreat.

Avoiding the fenced shafts of disused antimony mines, I made my way to Lundy Cove, one of my favourite places in the whole world. At low tide, its shore of golden sand fringed by colourful rocks and boulders becomes exposed. It's easy then to explore the rock pools, caves and other natural features, such as the dramatic natural arch called Lundy Hole, that make this such a magical spot. As a family, we often make the quarter-mile (0.4 km) trek from the National Trust car-park down to the cove, timing our outing to coincide with low tide. For anyone happy to be on a seashore away from ice-cream vans and other amenities, I highly recommend it.

Moving on towards Pentire Point, I recalled all the times that I have wandered along this stretch of coast. No matter what the weather, it has never failed to enthral me. It has almost everything that one would want on a coastal walk: a Point from which to view spectacular scenery; an island on which seabirds breed, and around which marine mammals and basking sharks often swim; a sea that seems to continue to the edge of the Earth; fascinating geological features, such as the high stacks of pillow lava – volcanic rock with holes formed during its explosive past; archaeological remains, especially those of the Iron Age fortress on the fishtail promontory called the Rumps, and a wealth of maritime wildlife.

The Jubilee Queen *takes visitors from Padstow to see seabirds on The Mouls.*

*Looking west towards Pentire Head.**

Wild thyme
(*Thymus polytrichus*)

A combination of relatively dry weather, fields managed non-intensively, and calcareous, mineral-rich soils, encourages the growth of a wide variety of plants around Pentire Point. A common and colourful member of the flora is wild thyme (*Thymus polytrichus*), which is attractive to insects.

Wild thyme, like the familiar garden variety, is heavily scented and sufficiently flavoursome to be a useful cooking herb. It owes its fragrance to oils packed in glands on its leaf surfaces. Crushing or nibbling the leaves ruptures the glands, and releases aromatic chemicals, chief among which is thymol. In its crystalline form, thymol is pure white and highly toxic. But diluted it is an effective antifungal agent and antiseptic. It also has anti-fermentation properties, and is used by bee-keepers to conserve honey.

Thyme has evolved its ability to produce smelly chemicals in order to attract useful insects, such as bees and other pollinators, and to deter harmful herbivores. But despite their potency, the chemicals fail to stop many plant-eaters – including sheep, rabbits, snails, and some insects – from using wild thyme as a food source.

One of the many insects that visit wild thyme plants is the meadow brown butterfly (*Maniola jurtina*, above). Another is the large blue butterfly (*Maculinea arion*), probably wild thyme's most notable associate.

The large blue has a complicated life cycle during which wild thyme, closely cropped turf, and a species of red ant play a crucial role. The butterfly became extinct on the North Cornwall coast in 1973, because there were not enough of these components in its habitat. Recently, it has been successfully reintroduced into another part of the North Cornwall coast, but the headland around Pentire Point has been managed for the benefit of a variety of wildlife, not only the large blue. Consequently, it lacks the large areas of closely cropped turf necessary to support the red ants essential for the successful reproduction of the butterfly.

At Pentire, I sat on the highest part of the Point and looked south down the mouth of the Camel Estuary towards Polzeath with its wonderful surfing beach, and then turned my gaze further up the estuary to Padstow and my home town of Wadebridge. I could just make out Cant Hill on the eastern bank of the Camel, between Padstow and Wadebridge. This has great significance as being the place from which our family name is derived. Our first documented ancestor had the surname of de Kant; in subsequent generations this changed to Cant, and then to Kent.

Tearing myself away from thoughts of genealogy, I strode down the familiar path to Polzeath via Pentire Glaze. My target was an ice-cream van on the beach, but before I could get to it I was accosted by two Wadebridge relatives, Bernard and Margaret Irons, who happened to be taking the sea air. They seemed a little puzzled as to why, on such a hot and sunny day, and only seven or so miles from home, I should be kitted out in long-distance walking shoes, and carrying a rucksack laden with wet-weather clothing and a tent. I did seem a bit overdressed compared to the swim-suited bodies on the sands of Hayle Bay. After a brief explanation, I got to the van and bought two cider ice lollies. Revived by their fantastically thirst-quenching and cooling effects, I continued purposefully along the cliff tops overlooking Greenaway and Daymer, then along the energy-sapping deep sands opposite Padstow, and reached Rock in the late afternoon.

There is much to see between Pentire and Rock and around the rest of the Camel Estuary. This is an Area of Outstanding Natural Beauty (AONB), and a Special Area of Conservation (SAC), with magnificent scenery, and a wide range of natural habitats teeming with wildlife. (For anyone wanting to find out more, I recommend *Exploring the Camel Estuary*, a little book which I compiled with Adrian Langdon.)

I whiled away the time waiting to catch the ferry from Rock to Padstow by exploring the shore. Among the plentiful marine life, mussels and their molluscan predator, the dogwhelk, dominated the wave-cut platforms.

Mussels and dogwhelks

Most of the mussels in the Camel are not the common British species (*Mytilus edulis*), but one of Continental origin (*Mytilus galloprovincialis*). The Gallic mussel is so prevalent on the shores towards the mouth of the estuary that it is called simply the Padstow Mussel.

Dotted among the mussels are dogwhelks (*Nucella lapillus*), with shells of varying colours and shades. The survival of dogwhelks, with such conspicuous shells, may be due to there being fewer shore crabs on the exposed shores of North Cornwall. On the sheltered shores of the south coast, where shore crabs are more plentiful, dogwhelks tend to be well camouflaged with drab, monochrome shells.

A dogwhelk has gruesome eating habits. It feeds on a mussel by making a hole through the bivalve's shell, partly by dissolving the shell with acidic chemicals, and partly by mechanically rasping the shell with its radula (a toothed, tongue-like structure). When drilling is completed, the dogwhelk pokes its proboscis through the hole and secretes digestive enzymes on to the soft flesh of the mussel. When the mussel's flesh has the consistency of soup, the dogwhelk sucks it up, using its proboscis as a straw. A dogwhelk usually spends at least a day eating a single mussel meal, and in some cases it takes as long as a week.

The harbour at Padstow.

After catching the ferry to Padstow, I went through the town, glancing in shop windows on my way. One of the shops I looked in was that of the Padstow Mussel Company, founded by my friend Susie Ray. Susie is not only a fine artist and designer, using the mussel as a motif on mugs and other crockery, but also an excellent and creative photographer. She has kindly contributed several photos to this book, including *Cornish Fruits de Mer* (opposite), which is particularly relevant to Padtow, the home of the National Lobster Hatchery and several fine restaurants that serve shellfish dishes.

I made my way to the library which Merryn manages. She drove me home for a much-needed bath, an excellent meal, a good book (she welcomes the business), and a very satisfying night's sleep.

Cornish Fruits de Mer

Some of the shellfish found around the Cornish coast.

Padstow to Trevelgue, Newquay

It was no easier leaving the comforts of home the second time than the first. Like a condemned man, I had a hearty breakfast, then Merryn drove me back to Padstow to continue my odyssey.

As I walked down to the harbour and along the Coast Path towards Stepper Point, I felt for a time as if I were floating on air. This was not the after-effects of drinking wine the previous evening, but because at home I had discarded about five pounds of inessential gear from my rucksack. Although this was a relatively small weight, it had become like the straw that was in danger of breaking the camel's back.

I didn't dawdle in Padstow. As it's part of my home territory, I frequently visit this ancient town and it never fails to charm me. I love to explore the narrow streets and the harbour, and to consider how things have changed since the Elizabethan adventurers Sir Francis Drake and Sir Walter Raleigh visited the port. Drake put in at Padstow in 1565 on his return from the West Indies, no doubt weighed down with pieces of eight which he offloaded in the local hostelries. Sir Walter Raleigh had a house here which he frequently used during his years as Warden of Cornwall. At this time, Padstow was

Windsurfers on Doom Bar.

one of the most important ports in England, with up to six shipbuilding yards. Among other vessels they produced were the famous Padstow schooners, renowned all over the world. Padstow's importance as a port declined with the advent of steam, and the encroachment of the estuary by the Doom Bar.

Doom Bar

Doom Bar, as the original name *Dun* (meaning sand) Bar implies, is a huge mass of sand. Over the years this has shifted from one side of the Camel Estuary to the other. Doom Bar now stretches from just off the cliffs near Hawker's Cove almost to Trebetherick Point, leaving only a narrow channel into the upper parts of the estuary at low tide. As with most frightening or dangerous natural phenomena, there is a legend attached to it: the Bar was created by a ferocious storm after a dying mermaid, fatally wounded by a young man of Padstow, cursed the town.

The Bar is a feature of the Estuary that requires respect from mariners who have to negotiate it. Over 300 boats, including three lifeboats, have been wrecked on its sand, and many lives lost. The most recent deaths were in 1997. A small boat put to sea in rough weather, despite warnings from the harbour master. Even though the coastguard was informed as soon as the boat left port, it overturned so quickly on the Doom Bar that nothing could be done to save the two men on board.

In June 2007, the crew of the Padstow Lifeboat spent 11 hours at sea rescuing two yachts and their crews. The crews of both yachts had to be airlifted to safety because of the danger of crossing the Doom Bar. Coxswain and lifeboat crew were commended for their actions and bravery, and the incident provoked much comment on the website of Yachting and Boating World. Proof, if proof were needed, that the Bar is still a threat to lives and shipping.

With the harbour behind me, I took the tarmac path up to the War Memorial at the summit above St Saviour's Point. The path is lined by countless benches, most placed in remembrance of people who loved this place. Looking at their labels made me feel a little melancholic, a feeling that grew when I reached the War Memorial. Its large, modern granite cross overlooks much of the Camel Estuary and the whole of Padstow – a fitting place for a memorial to those Padstonians who lost their lives during the two World Wars.

After pausing to make a silent prayer, I continued along the Coast Path down to St George's Cove, past the remnants of the Second World War gun emplacement at Gun Point, through the sand dunes behind Tregirls Beach, around Hawker's Cove and up to Stepper Point.

On the way I met a lady walking two labradors along the path. The dogs were off their leads and generally sniffing about. Suddenly, a grey squirrel with a death wish appeared from nowhere. Inevitably, the labs gave chase, but the squirrel escaped to taunt another day.

At Stepper Point, I took a short rest and a good, long drink of water to reduce the risk of further dehydration. When I made my short pit-stop at home, I weighed myself and found that I had lost 2 kilograms (4 pounds) in three days. I could afford to lose a bit of flab, but if I continued at that rate, I would be more than 9 kilograms (20 pounds) lighter by the end of my journey. However, it was not fat loss causing my weight reduction, but loss of vital water. I had to be more careful if I were not to become ill from dehydration, especially as the sun had come out and this, combined with a cooling breeze, would result in my losing water without even being aware of it.

During my short stop, I took a close look at the stone tower at Stepper. It was built in 1832 by the Association for the Preservation of Life and Property. Its purpose was to act as a day mark for vessels moving along the coast, especially those entering the Camel.

After my break, I rounded Stepper Point and veered south-west towards Trevone Bay. This is the first of many surfing beaches between Padstow and Newquay. Although they might look similar, each has its own unique identity, and its own group of *aficionados*. Keen surfers are usually quite fickle in their allegiance to a particular beach, and just 'follow the surf'. Subtle differences in the beaches may mean that when one is no good for surfing another is ideal.

Before reaching Trevone, I was surprised to see a giant hole in a grassy field, well away from the edge of the cliff. This curious, circular feature is called the Round Hole. It looks like a meteor-created crater, but is in fact a collapsed cave. I tried to photograph it but failed to capture a true sense of its size. As with many geological features, you really have to be there to appreciate its magnitude.

It's but a short distance from Trevone to Harlyn Bay. Though it may not look important now, in the Bronze Age Harlyn Bay was probably one of the cultural centres of Europe.

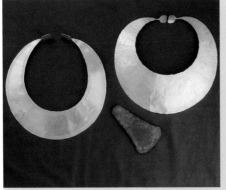

To get round Harlyn Bay, I walked along the beach as far as I could, then headed north-west on the path to Mother Ivey's Bay. Across the Bay I could see Padstow's new lifeboat station, with the latest Royal National Lifeboat Institution (RNLI) vessel sitting proudly on the slipway. The station was moved from the port in 1967 after three of its boats were lost on the Doom Bar. The new location gives the lifeboat speedy access to the open sea, yet it is protected from most storms by the Merope Rocks.

From Mother Ivey's Bay, I passed Trevose Head lighthouse (the first of the several that I was to see during my journey), carefully skirted another, smaller Round Hole, and dropped down to Booby's Bay and Constantine Bay.

Just beyond the high-water mark, and protected from the sea only by dunes, is Trevose Golf and Country Club. Not having carried my golf clubs on my trip, I had to wait until my return to play the course. But I did discover that it has one of the most spectacular and exposed fourth greens in the country. With nothing between it and North America, its flag flaps on even a calm day. In a storm, the green is covered in sea spray, while

Trevose golf course, looking towards Trevose Head.

the sound of the wind and waves makes shouts of 'fore!' irrelevant. Luckily, on the day I played conditions were relatively serene, and I managed to bogey my way around without losing even one ball: a rare occurrence indeed.

As I walked across Constantine Bay, I came across a board giving information about the locality. St Constantine's Church and Well were mentioned, but most of the information was about natural history. I read that the dunes require 'constant care… to ensure their long term conservation. Further work will be carried out by the North Cornwall Heritage Coast services and the Parish Council in the area to protect and extend the dune system.'

So after returning from my coastal rambles, I was greatly surprised to learn that plans had been submitted by the RNLI for a permanent lifeguard building in the middle of the dunes. These had progressed so far that only after last-minute local opposition was voiced at a final site meeting were the plans withdrawn. There was a great deal of sympathy for the RNLI, which has taken responsibility from the local council to safeguard the beaches. But there was a general feeling that the sand dunes and their wildlife should not be endangered by disturbances associated with building and maintaining a permanent structure right in the centre.

At the wave-cut platform that borders the southern edge of Constantine Bay was the familiar seaside sight of families armed with nets to sweep the rock pools, and buckets in which to place their quarry. An

The magnificent sweep of Constantine Bay.

The shanny (*Blennius pholis*)
Look in many of the rock pool crevices at low tide, and you will be confronted with a face-on view of the shanny (also known as the blenny). This delightful fish spends nearly all its life on the shore, mostly within a limited number of rock pools.

The shanny is well adapted to its way of life. Its scales are so deeply embedded in its skin that it feels smooth. Its fins and the roof of its mouth have an excellent blood supply, enabling their surfaces to be used for gaseous exchange; this allows the shanny to survive out of water for 24 hours or more, as long as its skin is kept moist.

The shanny's body surface is covered with pigmented spots, so it can change colour to fit its background, or signal its mood to other fish. When it feels aggressive it goes black with rage; but when in the mood for courtship it assumes a more colourful attire.

The adaptations of the shanny for life in rock pools make it an ideal aquarium fish. They are hardy and (for a fish) very intelligent – you can even train them to emerge on to a rock and take food from your hand.

occasional scream of delight indicated that a shanny or some other exciting form of marine life had been found.

I reached Treyarnon at about 2 p.m., in time to have a delicious ham and lettuce sandwich, and a pot of tea at the Youth Hostel. From there, I continued to Porthcothan, passing three Iron Age castles and a Royal Society for the Protection of Birds (RSPB) sanctuary on the way. As requested on a sign, I took care to keep to the footpath next to the sanctuary since the maritime grassland is being managed to encourage skylarks and corn bunting – birds once common but now becoming rare.

Rock-pooling at Constantine Bay.

The maritime grassland between Treyarnon and Porthcothan is rich in wildflowers, like yellow kidney vetch.

Porthcothan is where Nick Darke lived. Nick is probably best remembered as a playwright whose work reflected his two passions: Cornwall and the sea. But among the marine fraternity, Nick and his wife Jane are better known as experts on objects transported to the shores of North Cornwall by the Gulf Stream. Their numerous finds include hardwood and seeds from the tropics, and fish tags from Newfoundland. One type of seed worth special mention is the heart seed (*Entada gigas*). It is produced by a tropical bean that has the longest pod in the world. Some pods extend more than two metres. A single pod contains up to 15 shiny brown seeds. Each has a hollow cavity and a thick, woody covering which make it very buoyant and resistant to decay. The seeds are usually washed by torrential rains into streams and rivers and make their way into the sea. Heart seeds found on the strandline of Cornish beaches

The path down to Porthcothan beach.

have probably been drifting for months or even years in oceanic currents such as the Gulf Stream. Nick and Jane's discoveries of these and other seeds, made over many years, have been of great value in indicating changes in movements of the Gulf Stream, and are contributing to scientists' understanding of the effects of global warming.

Sadly, Nick Darke died in 2005, but Jane still lives in their house close to the beach, and regularly goes on to the shore to search for

*The heart seed (*Entada gigas*).*

tropical items, and to gain inspiration for her oil paintings. Her work includes seascapes, pictures of lobsters, fish, and flowers, and still lifes of beach finds.

Wanting to find a place to sleep before nightfall, I had no time to follow in the footsteps of Nick and Jane, but vowed to beachcomb Porthcothan on another day. When I did so in October 2007, I was particularly keen to find the violet sea snail (*Lanthina janthina*) and any other tropical items, but all I managed to get for my efforts were a couple of cuttlefish bones and some driftwood.

The violet sea snail
(*Lanthina janthina*)

The violet sea snail is a warm-water mollusc that lives upside down, attached to the under-surface of the ocean by a frothy mass of stiff bubbles. As its shell is very light, the snail can maintain this position without sinking, and is carried wherever currents and wind take it.

The snail's main food is the by-the-wind-sailor (*Velella velella*), a soft-bodied, jellyfish-like creature. It has a mass of tentacles hanging from a float, the top of which projects upwards like a sail. Both the snail and its prey are carried by the Gulf Stream. The snail acquires its striking purple coloration from the pigment in the soft parts of the by-the-wind sailor.

While floats of by-the-wind sailor are quite frequently stranded on the beaches of North Cornwall, sometimes in their thousands, the shells of the snail are much less commonly found. Rarer still, because of their fragility, are full-sized, intact adult shells. Most shells are found battered to smithereens after being thrown by surf against rocks.

The shell featured in the photograph is in Stella Turk's collection. Its rarity and beauty make it a much-treasured item. Stella is a naturalist, born in the Isles of Scilly but a long-term resident at Reskadinick, a small hamlet near Camborne. With her husband Dr Frank Turk, she established the Biological Records Unit which holds information about all types of wildlife in Cornwall. Among the many thousands of records she has helped to amass are those of the violet sea snail and the by-the-wind sailor – just two of the many items that have drifted on to the shores of North Cornwall. In 2003, Stella was awarded an MBE for her services to nature conservation.

I left Porthcothan along the path by the side of the beach, went past a small shop and post office, continued out towards Trescore Islands, cut back to Porth Meor, and then up to Park Head. The stretch between Porth Meor and Park Head is particularly well known for its birds. Two which frequent the area are peregrines and fulmars. Although I saw the distinctive white droppings of peregrines on the cliffs, I was not fortunate enough to catch sight of this bird in action.

Park Head, rising 65 metres (over 200 feet) out of the sea, commands fantastic views up and down the coast. It is not surprising that it is the site of an Iron Age castle dating from about the first century BC. Two defensive banks across its neck protect the headland, which was probably a permanent site.

The castle is not the only archaeological feature in the area. On my way from Park Head to Carnewas, I counted six Bronze Age barrows (burial mounds) poking above the landscape.

The walk between Park Head and the National Trust café at Carnewas is one of the easiest and most beautiful on the Cornish Coast Path. Each year, thousands tread the soft turf, kept immaculate by the Trust, aided

Bedruthan Steps – a series of remnant stacks. *

and abetted by hungry rabbits. Many people come in early summer to see wildflowers, such as sea pinks (thrift), in full bloom. But most come to see the impressive series of remnant stacks known as Bedruthan Steps.

In the days of steam locomotives, posters of the magnificent coastal scenery were displayed in carriages of Great Western Railway trains, making the Steps an icon of the Cornish Riviera.

I made a pit-stop at the National Trust café and shop at Carnewas, and then hurried as fast as my fatigued legs could carry me towards Newquay.

Sea pink (thrift), on a hedge.

I quickly descended into Mawgan Porth; scampered across its beach, stopping only to buy a reviving orange ice lolly, and then took the westbound path to Watergate Bay. Barely pausing to see the surfers displaying their skills at Watergate, and not having enough cash to sample the delights of Jamie Oliver's famous Fifteen restaurant, I pushed on to Trevelgue Head.

Queen Bess Rock and Samaritan Island

These are probably the best-known Steps at Bedruthan. Queen Bess Rock got its name from its profile, which was once similar to that of our first Queen Elizabeth. In 1912, Folliott-Stokes wrote in *The Cornish Coast and Moors* that it '... exhibits the well-known features of the Virgin Queen. The highly developed nose, the thin lips, the somewhat meagre bust...'. However, since he penned these words, the Rock has suffered a fate similar to that which the Queen inflicted on her cousin, Mary Queen of Scots. It has lost its head – but from storms rather than the blade of an executioner's axe.

Samaritan Island was named after the *Good Samaritan*, a ship of the East India Company wrecked on its rocky outcrops on 22 October 1846, at the height of the period known as The Hungry Forties because of the potato famine. The incident has gained considerable notoriety for the plundering of the ship's cargo by locals desperate for food and deprived of luxuries. Rumour has it that there was barely a home in the locality that did not have food, a piece of cloth, or an item of silverware from the wreckage.

Their response to the wrecking has been summed up in the following couplet:

The *Good Samaritan* came ashore
To feed the hungry and clothe the poor.

Unfortunately for many local men, the law enforcement agencies did not view their opportunistic actions in the same way, and many ended up in the County Jail at Bodmin.

Carnewas mine

The National Trust shop above Bedruthan Steps was originally the counting house (or offices) for the Carnewas mine, and the café was also converted from mine buildings. Not much is known of the venture. Shafts are shown in detail on old Ordnance Survey maps, and there is some evidence of surface workings. One report of mining in the region (H.G. Dines, *The Metalliferous Mining Region of South-West England*, HMSO, 1956) states that 940 tons of reddy-brown haematite (a source of iron) were raised between 1871 and 1874. But the historian A.K. Hamilton Jenkin believes lead and copper were the main objective. He suggests that the mine adits were entered from the beach or cliffs, and wonders if Bedruthan Steps took its name originally from the ladders needed to reach the mine workings.

The headland is the site of yet another promontory fort. Archaeological evidence, pottery and such-like, indicates that the site was occupied on and off from the early Iron Age to as late as the sixth century AD. Its headland position, cut off from the mainland by a series of seven ramparts, probably made it the most heavily defended Iron Age fort in Cornwall. It is also possible that the smelting of iron, which could be obtained from cliffs nearby, helped to make the community more self-sufficient.

Trevelgue Head – an Iron Age promontory fort
occupied until the sixth century AD.*

As I approached Trevelgue, I could see clearly some of the fort's defensive structures, revealed by shadows formed in the failing light of evening. Close-up, however, there is not much to see of this once-magnificent structure. Nevertheless, like many visitors, I enjoyed walking out to the edge of the promontory to look at Newquay and its seascape.

I would have liked to camp at Trevelgue Head and dream of its knights of old. But quite rightly, pitching a tent, even a tiny one, is prohibited, and I had to make do with an overnight stay in an official campsite a mile or so inland.

Day 5 (15.8 ml/25.3 km)

Trevelgue, Newquay to St Agnes Beacon

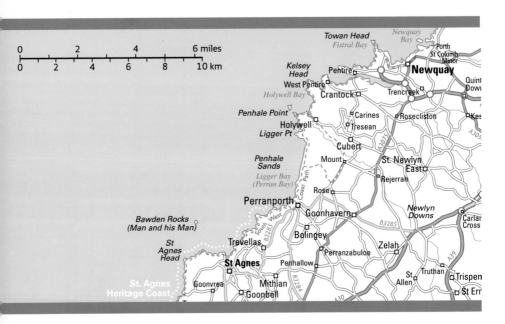

I had a very restless night. Perhaps I should have gone elsewhere when the camp receptionist warned me that I might be disturbed. I discovered that hundreds of university and college students were using the site for an end-of-year get-together. But I was too tired to bother finding another pitch, and put up my tent as far as I could from the mass of students.

When I'd arrived, it was pleasantly quiet. Little did I know that the young people were merely recharging their batteries before going out on the town. From about 1 a.m. until 3.30 a.m., my sleep was disrupted by groups of revellers returning from the nightclubs of Newquay. The final student interruption came when a group of lads, a little the worse for wear, took a short cut over the hedge into the camp and stumbled into my tent. Thankfully, no lasting damage was done. The students apologized for the unscheduled early morning wake-up call, and went off nursing their hangovers.

*My campsite at Newquay.**

As soon as the students had quietened down, the local bird population began to sing their dawn chorus. Dozing, but not able to get back into a deep sleep, I decided to get up just after 5 a.m., have a mug of tea, pack my tent away and start the fifth day of my walk.

When I left the site, it resembled a field at a pop festival: gear strewn all over the place, and great pyramids of beer cans piled on the ground in remembrance of the previous night's drinking.

With few regrets, I headed back to Trevelgue Head, where I had an impromptu (and blissfully quiet) breakfast of a couple of biscuits and a mug of tea. From Porth I took the Coast Path route past Lusty Glaze and across Barrowfield into Newquay Town.

Having worked in Newquay, I know the town quite well. I always enjoyed its beaches, or looking out to sea from its cliff tops, but this unashamed holiday town is not really my type of place.

Once a genteel holiday destination for families, Newquay has become a place of pleasure for the masses, its streets lined with bars, clubs and shops displaying garish plastic signs. It is also a great surfing centre.

I left Newquay town via its harbour, and took the Coast Path out to the whitewashed Lookout Hut on Towan Head. Then I skirted past the magnificent red-bricked Headland Hotel, and dropped down on to Fistral Beach.

Tolcarne Beach. The cliffs behind the beach form part of the seafront of Newquay, with its many hotels and guesthouses.

The Lookout Hut on Towan Head – ideal for observing seabirds.

From there, I trekked along the back of The Warren at Pentire and down Riverside Crescent, eventually finding Fern Pit Café, where I hoped to take the ferry across the Gannel. Unfortunately, it was only 8 a.m., and the ferry did not start until 10 a.m. And as it was close to high tide, the two tidal bridges – one just below the café and the other at the bottom of Trethellan Hill – were flooded. If I had been sensible, I would have waited there,

Fistral beach

Fistral is probably the most popular surfing beach in the British Isles. Although surf was not high when I walked across its sands, it can be huge when conditions are right. A low spring tide, a depression in the mid-Atlantic, combined with a certain type of wind can create a swell that crashes over the Cribber reef about a half mile (0.8 km) off shore to form a wave up to 9 metres (30 feet) high. Known simply as The Cribber, after the reef over which it is formed, this highly dangerous wave has been ridden only rarely. Plans have been submitted to build an artificial reef off Fistral to increase the frequency of huge waves.

had a leisurely second breakfast, and been ferried to Crantock beach with very little effort. But keen not to waste time, I decided to walk along the Gannel Road almost to the boating lake in Trenance Park, where I could use the third bridge to cross the river, and switch back along its southern bank to the beach. This tiresome detour of some three to four miles

Looking up the Gannel Estuary at low tide, when the bridge just below Fern Café is exposed.

(6 km) up and down the banks of the Gannel enabled me to reach Crantock only about a quarter of an hour before the first ferry.

From Crantock beach, I rounded Pentire Point West, missing the collapsed cave that can be seen from the lower path, and walked on to Porth Joke.

Porth Joke

Porth Joke, or Polly Joke as it is known locally, derives its name from the Cornish phrase *poll an chauk*, which means 'the chough's cove'. The chough referred to is the red-billed Cornish chough, now extinct around Newquay.

One of the great attractions of Porth Joke is its remoteness from cars and commercialism. The nearest carpark is more than a quarter of a mile away. Like all the land fringing the coast between Porth Joke and Holywell, it is owned by the National Trust. This land is sensitively managed to encourage wildlife. Sheep graze the headland, keeping it free from impenetrable scrub.

Low-intensity farming is carried out in the fields behind the beach, so that an enormous variety of increasingly rare arable weeds can flourish. For just a few weeks in June and July, and only in some years, the fields become ablaze with the red of three species of poppy and the yellow of corn marigolds. Other colourful flowers include field scabious, bugloss and, in spring, cowslips.

The presence of numerous wild flowering plants attracts a wealth of butterflies and moths, such as meadow browns, skippers, and the dramatically coloured six-spot burnet moth (*Zygaena filipendulae*, left).

Inside the cave in Kelsey cliffs is a basin of crystal-clear water, which I supposed to be the Holy Well.

Taking care not to frighten the grazing sheep, I walked out to Kelsey Head and round to Holywell Bay.

Two wells contend for the honour of giving Holywell its name: the Trevornick Valley well, between a quarter and a half of a mile (0.4–0.8 km) inland, and the Holywell well in a sea cave. I'm not familiar with the well in the valley, but I have explored the sea cave.

I tried to see the well during my perambulation of Cornwall, but failed to find it. I returned in September to make a second attempt, and discovered that the well is accessible only at low tide.

As the tide was not fully out when I arrived, I had to wade up to my waist through cold water to reach the part of the southern Kelsey cliffs in which the cave has been formed. Its entrance is an uninviting, narrow slit. I crawled through the slit and entered the dimly lit cave. Once my eyes had adjusted to the lack of light, I could see a slope lined with slimy green and brown algae. Slipping and sliding, I climbed the slope and entered the main chamber of the cave. On shining a light inside the grotto-like chamber, I was amazed to see a series of steps lined with creamy-white calcareous deposits tinted with red, blue and brown pigments – presumably from blue-green algae or bacteria. Mineral-rich water drips on to the steps creating pools. I clambered up to the top step, which has the deepest and largest basin, full of crystal-clear water, which I supposed was the Holy Well.

The well in the sea cave is marked on the Lanhydrock Atlas of 1694, and is thought to have been used for sacred purposes long before that. As Folliott-Stokes asked when he set eyes on this fantastic pool:

Is it to be wondered at that the imagination of the Middle Ages was caught by this strangely beautiful natural water supply, or that the priesthood of the time should have claimed for it miraculous healing powers?

I reached Holywell at 11 a.m., had a brunch (a tasty bacon sandwich helped down by a pot of tea), and then took the footpath to Perranporth. I followed the path around the perimeter of Penhale army camp, keeping to the right of the white marker posts, then walked down to Ligger, or Perran Bay.

From Ligger Point, the view of the bay and its hinterland is dominated by the magnificent dunes. These are probably the largest, least modified and most diverse dunes in Cornwall.

I had no time to explore. As the tide was out, I took the short cut across the sands to Perranporth. This is easier than taking one of the many paths through the dunes, but not as interesting. It was almost sacrilegious for a Cornishman to go past the dunes without visiting what is thought to be the last resting place of St Piran, the patron saint of tinners, and probably the most revered saint in Cornwall. As a penance, I made a pilgrimage to the dunes soon after completing my 16-day walk.

A place of pilgrimage

Honoured in the names of Perranporth (Port of Piran) and the hamlet of Perranzabuloe (Piran in the Sand) among others, St Piran is the patron saint of tinners and Cornish miners. He is undoubtedly Cornwall's best loved saint. In legend, he had worked in Wales and Ireland, and was already quite old when he reached Cornish shores. He arrived from Ireland after some disgruntled local leaders took a dislike to his influence, his miracles and his piety, and threw him into a stormy sea tied to a millstone. Fortunately for Piran and the Cornish, the millstone miraculously floated; the storm died down, and St Piran calmly floated to his new homeland. Here he built a small oratory for preaching and prayers. The current oratory dates from the sixth century, and is one of the oldest Christian buildings in Britain.

According to tradition, St Piran was buried at the oratory when he died, but was later exhumed and various body parts distributed as relics. The saint's head was kept at the new church, built to replace the oratory. In 1835, a headless skeleton is said to have been found buried under the oratory's altar, leading to speculation that this might be the body of the saint. Sadly, the oratory itself is now buried for its own protection under a concrete casing and a mound of earth, but the spot is still worth a visit for a moment of quiet contemplation.

The oratory had to be abandoned when it was overwhelmed by sand, and around the time of the Norman conquest a new church was built a little further inland. This church was protected from the encroaching sand by a small stream. The remains of the building can still be seen among the dunes. Although St Piran's Cross marks the site of the church's graveyard, the cross appears to be more ancient than the oldest surviving parts of the church. The new church grew, and by the fourteenth century was a place of pilgrimage.

Even this church was not safe from the sand for ever. Mine working caused the stream to dry up, and once again St Piran's church was threatened with burial. Eventually, the decision was made to leave the church and even its graveyard to the sand. A third church was built at nearby Perranzabuloe. The old church was dismantled so the stone could be used in the new church, and by 1805 this was ready for use. The old site has not been entirely abandoned. Now, new pilgrims come to celebrate St Piran's Day (5 March).

The Cross of St Piran

The magnificent three-holed granite cross stands on the dunes, just a few metres from the remains of the Norman church, the second of the religious sites associated with St Piran. The origins and age of the cross are not known, but some experts believe it to be the cross mentioned in a document of AD 960. It may be considerably older than that.

The site is one of the most atmospheric in Cornwall. Looking out from here across the medieval churchyard and dunes, some would claim a greater sense of the past than anywhere else in Cornwall.

The hermitage cell in a cliff at Perranporth.

I reached Perranporth early in the afternoon, and scouted around the beach. On its extreme southern edge, I came across what looked like a hermitage cell carved into the top of one of the rocks. The entrance to the cell was guarded by a half-open old wooden door that was coming off its thick metal hinges. From this curiosity, I climbed the adjacent steps up to the cliff top. After walking a short distance along a road, I rejoined the Coast Path to Cligga Head.

Here the path passes through the spoil heaps of a number of abandoned tin and copper mines. Most of the mines flourished for only a few years in the nineteenth century.

When I reached Trevellas Porth, the tide was still low enough for me to clamber over the rocks

Mine caps and bats
The disused mine shafts around St Agnes have been covered with conical mesh caps, mainly to prevent animals and people from plummeting down into them. But the caps have also been designed to allow bats, including the rare greater horseshoe, to move freely in and out of the shafts.

Gloriously coloured rocks and an unpolluted sea at Trevaunance Cove.

to Trevaunance Cove, just as Folliott-Stokes had done at the beginning of the twentieth century. Whereas I enjoyed looking down on to gloriously coloured rocks and an unpolluted sea, Folliott-Stokes' experience was very different. In his book *The Cornish Coast and Moors*, he writes first about Trevellas Cove, and then about Trevaunance Cove:

> Here the once pellucid brook is almost black, stone walls instead of flowers line its banks, and its befouled waters darken the sand in the cove and discolour the sea for several yards from the shore. Clambering over some rocks we soon reach Trevaunance Cove, where things are still worse. On the beach itself a great over-shot wheel revolves, and discharges dirty water on to the already discoloured sand. On the hill-side above are more wheels, slowly-moving chains, mud heaps, and smoking chimneys; while the loud and ceaseless clatter of stamps fills the air with noise. This valley, before man polluted it, must have been a very beautiful one...

Thankfully, although in many ways it's sad that mining has ceased, the valley is once again a very beautiful one. It is also much quieter.

At Trevaunance Cove, I saw more remnants of St Agnes' mining past. A mass of rectangular granite blocks lay strewn along the western side of the beach. These were once part of the harbour constructed to ship tin out of the town. The harbour was so important to trade that whenever

The path leading up to St Agnes Head.

damaged by storms, it was repaired. Sometimes it had to be almost completely rebuilt. When tin mining ceased, so did the reason for rebuilding the harbour.

From the pub above the beach, I found my way out of Trevaunance and climbed the path towards St Agnes Head. I paused at Newdowns Head to observe the sea birds. The cliffs here have probably the largest colony of kittiwakes (page 146) in Cornwall.

Before progressing further, I studied my map and went in search of the campsite at Beacon Cottage Farm. Relying on my extraordinary skills of navigation, I once again became completely lost, until a couple of kind locals pointed me in the right direction. Exhausted and hungry, I found the farm and settled down for the night.

Day 6 (23.6 ml/37.9 km)

St Agnes Beacon to Carbis Bay

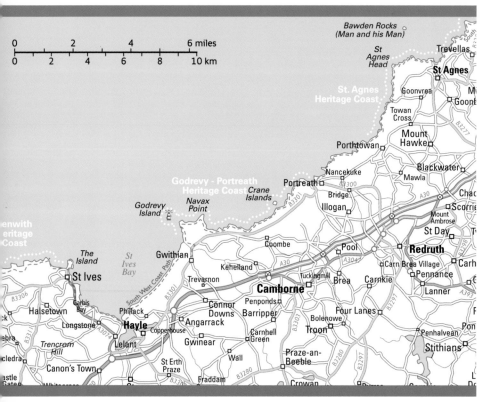

I woke with the birds just after 4 a.m., peeked out of my tent to absorb the outstanding sea views, and reflected on my luck at having such a wonderful start to the day. After a quick breakfast and a weather report from the very helpful camp staff, I set out on my sixth day's walk.

I had not gone far towards Wheal Coates before I met a man walking his dog around St Agnes Head. But when they headed inland, I had the ruins of the mine all to myself. I stopped to take advantage of the early morning sun, and photographed one of the buildings.

Towanroath Engine House, part of Wheal Coates.

The area around Wheal Coates is noted not only for its industrial archaeology, but also for its natural history. I was not lucky enough to see

Wheal Coates

The first written record of mining at Wheal Coates is dated 1692. But tin mining was undoubtedly carried out in the area long before that. On the cliff top, many trenches and pits, most now covered with heather and gorse, are probably the remains of medieval tin workings. The direction and depth of the trenches follow the tin- and copper-bearing veins or 'lodes' that were much sought after by the Cornish miners. The depth of the open-cast mining was limited by problems of removing flood water and raising the ore to the surface. It was only after the introduction of steam-driven pumping and winding gear that these problems could be solved satisfactorily, allowing really deep mining to take place.

The most striking ruins at Wheal Coates are the stamps and whim engine house, and the Towanroath pumping house built between 1872 and 1873. They housed the world-famous Cornish beam engines made by Harvey & Co. at Hayle. While the Towanroath engine pumped water out of the 600-foot (200-metre) Towanroath shaft, the stamp and whim engine raised and crushed the ore so it could be processed in nearby calciners; these create tin concentrate by driving off unwanted impurities, especially arsenic. The walls of several calciners can be seen close to the engine house.

The stamps and whim engine house represent the final phase of tin mining at Wheal Coates. In 1844 the mine was sold, and allowed to flood. It was exploited again in 1872, but only intermittently thereafter. A fall in the price of tin in the late 1880s led to its closure. An attempt to reopen it in 1911 was unsuccessful, but some locals believe that the land around Wheal Coates still conceals a wealth of unworked tin.

the peregrine falcons that patrol its skies. Nor did I catch a glimpse of the slow worms, adders or lizards that might have caused the rustling sounds I heard in the undergrowth. But I did see rock pipits and raven feeding among the ruins, and the bell heather (*Erica cinerea*) and western gorse (*Ulex gallii*) that make up much of the heathland.

There are several paths around Wheal Coates. I chose one that took me down to the coastal path in front of one of the most dramatically sited buildings in Cornwall, the Towanroath shaft head with its engine house. From there, I continued to the steep-sided cove of Chapel Porth.

I stopped to refill my water bottle, and had a quick look around the rocky shore in the cove. I was particularly keen to see the limpets that my friend Roger Burrows had told me about.

Roger lives at St Agnes, where he and his wife run a field studies centre. In the 1980s, we jointly ran a Natural History course for Exeter University's extra-mural department. I recall during one coffee break Roger telling me about his limpet observations. At the time, I was astonished when he described these lethargic-looking molluscs as being actively aggressive when attacked. I had thought that a limpet's only possible defence was to clamp down on to a rock and passively retreat under its shell.

Since hearing Roger's account of the limpets, I have read reports of similar observations in scientific literature. I now realize that limpets are not the docile creatures I once thought them to be.

I left the potentially violent limpets and walked the very narrow path past more disused mines and spoil heaps to Porthtowan. I didn't stop at this small resort, despite its pleasant-looking sand dunes and surfing beach, but carried on the path towards Portreath.

Common limpet (*Patella vulgata*)

The mineral-like encrustation on the limpet shell is a growth of the calcareous seaweed, *Lithothamnion*. The limpet (*Patella vulgata*) is one of the commonest marine molluscs. Out of water, it spends much of the time with its heavy triangular shell clamped tightly on to its home scar – an indentation in the rock in which the edge of its shell fits exactly.

When submerged, or sufficiently moistened, the limpet moves slowly but purposefully about, rasping the surface of rocks with the shovel-like teeth of its radula hardened with iron. It scrapes off diatoms, algae and anything else it can ingest. In so doing, it creates a 'garden', or bare patch of rock around its home scar.

If attacked, by a starfish or carnivorous whelk, for example, the limpet raises its shell quite high above the rock and waves it from side to side. This behaviour is described as 'mushrooming'. Sometimes the limpet will follow the 'mushrooming' by 'stomping' – suddenly smashing down the edge of its shell on to the intruder. Both forms of aggression may dislodge or deter an attacker.

Heath scorched black by a gorse fire at Portreath. *

After using the steps installed by the Royal Engineers on the steep-sided valley leading to Sally's Bottom, I reached the perimeter fence of RAF Portreath and what was once Nancekuke Chemical Defence Establishment (CDE).

For the mile or so I walked alongside the fence, I couldn't help feeling intimidated by its presence. Sometimes the fence hugs the path so closely that coastal walkers have only a metre or so between it and the cliff edge. My feelings weren't helped by the large, sinister-looking dome in a field

Nancekuke's secret past

Nancekuke held few secrets until the Second World War and the Cold War years that followed. In the relative peace of the pre-war years, much of Nancekuke was used as farmland. In 1940, all this changed. The land was requisitioned and used as an RAF Fighter Section Station and Overseas Air Dispatch Unit. Spitfires, Halifaxes, Blenheims and Mosquitoes were among the aircraft that flew from its four runways.

Between 1945 and 1950 it housed nothing more deadly than a Transport Command Briefing School and the Polish Resettlement Air Corps. But in May 1950, RAF Portreath was acquired by the Ministry of Supply as a CDE. Between 1954 and 1956, one of its functions was to develop and produce a nerve agent known as sarin. From then until the 1970s, Nancekuke CDE produced CS gas and other riot control agents.

In 1976, decommissioning of Nancekuke CDE began, and stocks of chemical agents were destroyed or transferred to Porton Down. The Establishment closed in 1980, and was formally handed back to the RAF on 30 September that year.

Since May 1997, when the activities of the site were declared under the terms of the Chemical Weapons Convention, the site has been open to inspection, and a major clean-up programme carried out.

Portreath

Though not the most attractive coastal town in Cornwall, Portreath's beach and rock pools are pleasant enough, and the harbour is interesting. It was built and extended by the Bassett family in the eighteenth century, and was made long and narrow to take full advantage of the protection provided by cliffs on the northern flank of the beach. During the height of the tin and copper mining, the harbour made Portreath an important port. Schooners shipped the ore to South Wales for smelting, returning to Portreath with cargoes of coal. During this period, few came to Portreath for holidays because much of its seafront was taken up by large stacks of coal.

The fish palace, now the site of the car-park, is evidence of a once-thriving pilchard industry. In the 1890s, the industry declined because the small, wooden seine-fishing boats were superseded by larger, steam-driven vessels, which preferred to use the less hazardous port at Hayle.

behind the fence; nor by having to walk through heath scorched black by a gorse fire, or the knowledge that Nancekuke CDE has a somewhat secret and dark past.

Today, Nancecuke CDE is no more. The airfield has only one active runway, which is used by Royal Air Force (RAF) and Royal Navy helicopters. The large dome in the field is a radome (a structure designed to protect radar-tracking equipment from the elements), and much of the maritime heath is designated a Site of Special Scientific Interest (SSSI) because of its wildlife value.

As I approached Portreath, I found that the Coast Path was closed because the nearby cliff had crumbled away. I was diverted along a road, and reached the harbour at about 10.30 a.m. After a quick look around the harbour, I refuelled with an excellent brunch of scrambled eggs and tea at the Harbourside Bistro.

From the restaurant, I made my way through the town along the main road and back to the Coast Path. The long stretch between Portreath and my next stop at Hell's Mouth is known locally as the North Cliffs. It is easy and pleasant walking, mainly along well-managed paths through open heath dominated by gorse. Although slightly hazy, the views of the mile after mile of magnificent coastal scenery were still breathtaking.

I reached the Hell's Mouth car-park and its café at about 1.30 p.m., had a drink and a quick bite to eat, and then went a short distance to the deep cleft to find out why it has been given such an awe-inspiring name. Taking care not to get too close to the crumbling edge of the high and precipitous cliffs, I peered down on to a swirling sea that crashed against treacherous rocks and boomed into caves that are deep and dark. I left thinking the name well deserved.

From Hell's Mouth, I went north-west towards Navax Point, ignoring the paths down to Smuggler's Cove and Fishing Cove on the way.

The caves at Hell's Mouth are deep and dark.

The caves below the Point are favourite breeding places for grey seals, but I pressed on to the cliffs around Mutton Cove (near Godrevy Head), where I knew I would have a good chance of seeing the seals at fairly close range.

I was not disappointed. When I arrived at the cliffs, I joined a group of holiday-makers and looked down into the cove. Its little beach was packed with seals. Motionless, they looked very much like the boulders among which they lay. As well as seals on the beach, there were several in the near-by water. As if to delight their audience, they were putting on a fine display of bobbing and cavorting about.

Mutton Cove, its beach packed with seals.

Grey seal
(Halichoerus grypus)
The grey seal is the largest British mammal breeding on land. A female grows up to 1.75 metres (nearly 6 feet) in length and 150 kilograms (330 pounds) in weight. Adult males are considerably bigger, being up to 3 metres (nearly 10 feet) in length and 250 kilograms (550 pounds) in weight.

Agile in water but cumber-some on land, grey seals come to the shores of North Cornwall to breed, mainly in autumn. The relatively remote sea-caves between Godrevy Head and Hell's Mouth are among the females' favourite breeding places. They crawl deep into the darkest part of the cave, well above high water, to give birth to their young. After being weaned and having their first moult, the white-coated pups experience a brief period of star-vation before they leave the protection of the cave and fully enter the sea.

Grey seals are much loved by most people, but not by all. Many fishermen be-lieve that seals make a significant contribution to the depletion of fish stocks. Others claim that seals damage fishing nets and follow the fishing boats, causing shoals to disperse. With the grey seal population increasing, the fishing industry has called for a cull. Seals are threatened not only by fishermen, but also by marine debris and pol-lution, especially oil pollution.

In recent years, much of our understanding of Cornish grey seals has come from Stephen Westcott. He is known as the Seal Man, not for his super-hero qualities, but because he has spent so much time studying the movements and habits of this loved but threatened mammal. Much of his work involved paddling his sea-kayak close to seals in open water, and using it to enter the sea-caves in which they breed.

I have had the privilege of joining Stephen on one of his seal-watching trips be-tween Godrevy Head and Navax point. Thankfully, our trip was cliff-based rather than one of Stephen's water-borne expeditions. He is one of those rare individuals who are truly passionate about their work, and is very keen to share his knowledge about the natural history of the seal, its plight, and the wonderful marine world in which it lives. A book of his thoughts and observations, *The Grey Seals of the West Country*, is published by the Cornwall Wildlife Trust (CWT).

From Mutton Cove, it was a short walk to Godrevy Head. Whenever I am here, I spend some time looking across at the lighthouse on Godrevy Island. It must be one of the most photographed lighthouses in Britain.

Turning from Godrevy Head to go towards Hayle, I crossed the Red River and, as the tide was out, took the long but direct route across the hard sand of the beach. I was glad to avoid walking through the Tow-ans (dunes) of Gwithian. Although the 'official' route of the Coast Path is through the dunes, it is almost impossible to distinguish it from the maze of other sandy tracks.

When I reached the entrance to Hayle Harbour, the tide was still low, and I was tempted to wade the short distance across the narrow outflow of the estuary to Porthkidney Sands. It was only a few paces, but with

Godrevy Island. The lighthouse may have inspired Virginia Woolf.

Virginian Woolf's lighthouse

Although close to the mainland, Godrevy lighthouse sits on a nearby island often thrashed by violent seas. Many fans of Virginia Woolf also believe it to be the lighthouse that inspired one of her most widely read and critically scrutinized novels, *To the Lighthouse.*

Although the book is set in the Hebrides, and has fictional as well as autobiographical components, there is little doubt that the novel draws on Virginia Woolf's early experiences. As a child, she made frequent visits to her family's holiday home, Talland House, above Porthminster Beach on the edge of St Ives. From there she could look across the three and a half miles (5.6 km) of the bay and see in the distance Godrevy lighthouse. It was built in 1859 after many lives had been lost from ships wrecked on a submerged reef near the island.

the water flowing fast and deep in places, it would have been stupid to attempt a crossing. In the autumn, when Merryn and I returned to take photographs, we saw another means of bridging the gap between the two sides of the harbour entrance: kite-surfers were taking advantage of a relatively calm sea and a strong wind to skim across the water.

In June, with no kite-surf board or boat handy, I had to walk to Porthkidney Sands, mainly by road. I plodded remorselessly through Hayle and around its harbour, then behind the Lelant Saltings, until a couple of hours and five miles (8 km) later, I reached Lelant Golf course.

If you make this journey, don't do as I did. Disappointed at having to turn my back on the sea, I deviated neither to the left nor the right of the official Coast Path, and made a determined effort to get this bit of road walking done with as quickly as possible. It was a mistake. When I returned

Hayle harbour looking towards the viaduct.

Hayle harbour
The harbour includes a quay that leads up to the viaduct, beyond which was the Harvey Foundry. When I scouted around the harbour, there were only small fishing boats and pleasure craft moored on the silty mud. But in Hayle's industrial heyday, the harbour was deeper and busy with ships bringing in coal to fuel the heavy industries, and taking out tin, copper and manufactured iron products from the Harvey Foundry. The administrative centre of the Harvey Foundry was in the building with the twin-clock tower, still prominent in Foundry Square. Before the standardization of British time, one of the clock faces gave London time while the other gave Cornish time.

Kite-surfers at Hayle.

to look around Hayle early in 2008, I did so at a much more leisurely pace, and realized how much I'd missed the previous summer.

Although today many people know Hayle for its three miles of golden sands and its proximity to the restaurants and art galleries of St Ives, in the eighteenth and nineteenth centuries it was a powerhouse of Cornish Industry. At the hub was the Harvey Foundry, just beyond the viaduct, and the harbour that leads up to it.

John Harvey, a blacksmith, started the iron foundry in 1779. But it was his son Henry who developed it as one of the finest in the land, and put Hayle on the map. Henry became a tycoon of national eminence, involving Harvey & Co. in a wide range of businesses, including ship-building, trading in tea and other merchandise, and rope-making, as well as ironmongering. The most famous products of the foundry were huge and highly efficient steam engines, which became known as the Cornish engines. Two – the largest

The Ropeworks
In upper Millpool, not far from Foundry Square, are the remnants of buildings used to manufacture rope for Harvey & Co. The buildings included a hemp and hatching house where the basic materials to make the rope were stored; a machine shop in which fibres were spun into long strands of white yarn; a boiler house which provided the steam that drove the spinning machines, and a capstan and despatch house where coils of rope were wound on to a capstan and then stored ready for despatch. The right-hand side of the Ropewalk still exists for almost its full length of over 90 metres (100 yards) from the Capstan House. Set in the wall at regular intervals are many of the iron sockets that supported the metal frames which separated the lengths of rope being manufactured.

in the world – were used to drain a Dutch lake, pumping nearly a million tons (907,000 tonnes) of water a day.

I reached the golf course at Lelant, and crossed one of the fairways to cries of 'Fore!', escaping the danger of being hit by wayward golf balls by taking the path next to the railway line above Porthkidney beach.

My final destination of the day was a campsite marked on my map as being at Chy-an-Gweal, near Carbis Bay. After several unsuccessful attempts at finding the site, I asked a local who told me the campsite no longer existed. Dropping his heavy Tesco bags, he pointed to the nearby superstore and told me it had replaced the campsite. It was only then that I checked the date on my map, and saw that it was printed in 1995 – another example of my meticulous pre-journey planning.

Unable to persuade Tescos to allow me to pitch my tent in or even near their store, I was determined to gain some advantage from my situation, so bought some bread, wine, olives and cheese, before hunting down the nearest guesthouse with vacancies.

St Elwyn's Church
Probably the boldest statement of the nineteenth-century prosperity brought to Hayle by the industrial activities of Harvey & Co. is the solidly built, granite edifice of St Elwyn's Church. One of the most prominent features in the town, it overlooks Copperhouse Pool and rises above the houses where Hayle Terrace meets Penpool Terrace. The church was created by John Sedding, the designer of the Brompton Oratory. It was begun in 1886 and completed two years later. It has some very fine stained glass windows, including the Friendship Window – a memorial to its first vicar, William Hosburgh, and his life-long friends, Frank and Anne Harvey, part of the dynasty that ran the company.

Carbis Bay to Pendeen

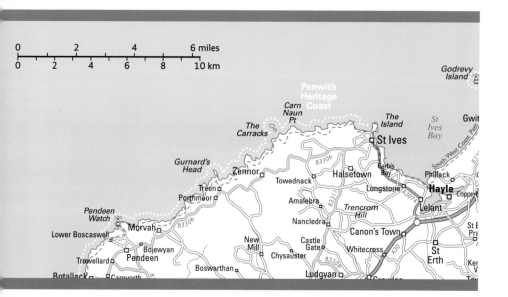

Smeaton's Pier

The rubble-and-masonry pier on the east side of the harbour entrance was designed in 1766 by John Smeaton, the engineer who built the famous Eddystone Lighthouse that now stands proudly on Plymouth Hoe as Smeaton's Tower. Thomas Richardson – Smeaton's foreman mason for the Eddystone Lighthouse – built the pier. The original length of 100 metres (330 feet) was completed in 1770. The pier used about 32,000 tonnes (35,000 tons) of stone and cost £9,408. In the late 1890s, it was extended a further 90 metres (300 feet).

The guesthouse I stayed in overnight did not offer breakfast, but I thought that lighting my Trangia stove in the bedroom might be frowned on, so I left early, and sauntered down the hill into St Ives to find a café, enjoying picture-postcard views of the harbour on the way.

After an excellent cooked breakfast, I walked towards the end of Smeaton's Pier to look at the harbour, on my way sneaking a look through the windows of the little Chapel of St Leonard.

St Ives in the early-morning sun. The light reflects off a sea that almost completely surrounds the town, giving it a distinctly Mediterranean look.*

St Leonard and his chapel

The plain and simple chapel at the start of Smeaton's Pier now houses a collection of model ships. From medieval times until the second half of the nineteenth century it was used by local fishermen. Here they would pray before setting out to sea. Once safely back in port, they rewarded the chaplain with fish from their catch.

St Leonard was a sixth-century Frankish nobleman, who rejected wealth and status for the peace and solitude of a monastery. His cult became popular from the eleventh century after an admirer wrote the story of his life. Many places of worship were built and dedicated to the saint at about the time that St Ives acquired this chapel – from Spain and Italy in southern Europe, to Bohemia and Poland in the north. The little chapel in St Ives probably marks the furthest west that the cult reached.

St Leonard is not a typical choice of patron saint for fishermen: he is associated with childbirth and the release of prisoners. Perhaps the fishermen of St Ives adopted him because of his humility and his desire for the simple life, but more likely it was because they wanted his protection against capture and enslavement by pirates or corsairs.

The *Cintra* anchor
The large, rusty sea anchor embedded in the pier was recovered from the *Cintra*, one of four ships wrecked in St Ives Bay in the great storm that struck the coast on 18 November 1899. The storm was so severe that the lifeboat couldn't be launched. Of the 12 crew, seven drowned but the other five were rescued by breeches buoy from Carbis Bay Beach and Carrack Gladden Cliff.

*The rocky start of the Coast Path west of St Ives.**

*The boulder-strewn ruggedness of the moors on the way to Zennor.**

When I reached the beginning of the pier, I examined the anchor recovered from the *Cintra*, then progressed to the end, sat close to the lighthouse, and shared a short time with the seagulls, just sitting and enjoying the harbour scene.

Although I could easily have spent the whole day, if not several days, exploring the harbour and narrow streets of St Ives, I had to get to Pendeen before evening. I didn't even have time to go into the Tate St Ives. I had visited it before, and have an abiding memory of listening to the taped recordings of Peter Lanyon and other great artists describing how they were inspired by the sea around St Ives, and its ever-changing moods. I would have enjoyed going again, to sit in the large atrium and look out of its giant windows on to Porthmeor Beach. Consoling myself that there would be other opportunities to visit the gallery, I proceeded to the Coast Path and started the seventh day of my walk.

The first half a mile (0.8 km) or so out of St Ives is easy walking, on short and bouncy turf. But I recalled that *The South West Coast Path Guide* rated the Coast Path from St Ives to Pendeen as 'severe', and the *National Trail Guide* referred to it as 'testing'. I was therefore not surprised when the pleasant path was transformed, as if by some curse, into a well-worn, boggy and rocky track. Someone had

A clear stream on the cliff between St Ives and Zennor. *

considerately placed broken paving stones to make the going easier, but there was still the continual risk of tripping if you didn't look where you were going.

If asked what I can remember most about my walk to Zennor, it would not be the magnificent seascapes at Pen Enys Point and Carn Naun Point, nor the gorse-covered, boulder-strewn ruggedness of the moors, for I could admire these only when I stopped. It would be the few metres of path just in front of my feet.

The walking was made even tougher by the weather. I would hate to give the impression that I'm one to complain about what most people would describe as a glorious summer's day, but it was hot and clammy, with not even a slight breeze to cool the brow. Rounding the wind-sheltered sides of the cliffs was sweaty work. Wetting my head in the clear water of the streams that flowed down the cliffs from the moors provided some relief, but this was short-lived, and I was soon sweating again.

Wilting and foot-sore, I decided to take a rest, well-earned or not, near The Carracks, and looked out for seals which are often in the area. I glimpsed a couple in the sea and hoped that the day-trippers in the boat going around The Carracks were equally fortunate.

Lazing about on the soft, grassy slopes, I got out my transistor radio, tuned into the test match (England *versus* West Indies, England 76 for 1), and tried to work out what I felt about this part of the Cornwall Coast Path. After considerable deliberation, I concluded that it was, to paraphrase

Seals are often seen near The Carracks.*

Wayside Folk Museum, Zennor
This is reputedly the oldest privately owned museum in Britain. Even before entering, there's much to see, including an iron water-wheel, dated c. 1860; the head of a ninth-century cross found in the hedge of a farm at Wicca, and the Zennor Plague Stone. During epidemics, such as those of cholera in 1832 and 1849, this stone had its central depression filled with vinegar so money could be cleaned before changing hands between villagers and outsiders. Inside, the museum contains a treasure trove of locally found artefacts – over 5,000 of them, dating from 3000 BC.

Dickens, 'the best of places and the worst of places.' The best because its rugged remoteness made me feel more at one with nature and the environment than anywhere else on the Coast Path; the worst because its uneven, rocky path and boulder-strewn slopes made walking, especially with heavy gear, very tough and at times extremely tiresome.

My next stop was the tiny hamlet of Zennor for a late lunch. To get there, I had to leave the path and go inland for a half mile (0.8 km) or so. The sandwich and cooling pint of shandy (anything more alcoholic would have made me feel even more dehydrated) I had at the Tinners Arms made the diversion worthwhile. On my way back to the Coast Path, I only had time to glance at the church and museum, but they looked so interesting that I made a note to return with Merryn to explore them more thoroughly.

The church of St Senara, Zennor

The present church at Zennor dates from the twelfth century, and stands on what was probably the site of an earlier Celtic Christian building. The most famous feature of the present church is the wooden mermaid chair. It was made by putting two bench ends together to make a chancel seat, and on the outer face of one end is carved a mermaid. On the tower, depicted on a dial, is another mermaid, with the inscription 'The glory of the world passeth. Paul Quick Fecit, 1737'.

According to local legend, the strong association between the church and mermaids is because one of the mythical sirens of the sea became so entranced by the singing of a local young man, Matthew Trewella, that she went to Zennor church to hear him. Another, less fantastic, reason for the association is given in an interesting note displayed in the church:

'Mermaid Chair'

But why have a Mermaid's chair in a church? Before the Christian era mermaids were one of the symbols for Aphrodite, goddess of the sea and of love. In one hand she held a quince (a love apple) and in the other a comb. Later the quince was changed to a mirror, symbol of vanity and heartlessness. In the Middle Ages, when Cornish mystery plays were performed, the mermaid was used as a symbol to explain the two natures of Christ. She was both human and fish, He was both man and God. Mermaid frescoes are found in other Cornish churches – Breage, Poughill, and Altarnun – but Zennor is the only one with a carving. The mermaid reminds us that St Senara also came by sea and founded a church in Zennor more than 1,400 years ago.

There are many other things of interest inside this wonderful church. Those that fascinated me most were the embroidered kneelers. Unless I miscounted them, there are 101. The embroideries include emblems, religious pictures, coats of arms, and local scenes.

Outside, on the south wall of the church, is a tablet dedicated to John Davey, allegedly the last person with traditional knowledge of the Cornish language. This claim may seem at odds with the more generally accepted claim that Dolly Pentreath of Mousehole, who died in 1777, was the last person who conversed in ancient Cornish. There may or may not be a difference between having 'considerable traditional knowledge' and 'conversing in' a language. In any case, the date at which a language no longer remains living is difficult to pinpoint.

Gurnard's Head, the promontory whose profile looks so much like the fish after which it is named. *

Red gurnard (*Trigla cuculus*)
The red gurnard is a handsome species, described by a first-time observer as looking like a cute, underwater puppy. Its unmistakable pectoral fins, chunky shape, red back and silvery belly make it one of the easiest fish to identify.

The red gurnard is a bottom-feeding fish. Sensing the sand with its finger-like rays, it moves lazily over the sea bed searching for prey. The gurnard is often caught with other bottom-feeders in the inshore waters around Cornwall.

Once regarded as unfit for consumption, it was usually thrown back with other unwanted members of the by-catch, or used in pots as bait for crabs and lobsters. But with stocks of many commercial fish declining, the sweet, nutty taste of the gurnard's pink, firm flesh is becoming more popular. It is increasingly finding its way on to the menus of the many fine fish restaurants in Cornwall. One particularly tasty way of preparing gurnard is to grill it with a little olive oil and Cajun spice.

At Zennor Head, I took the path that skirts Pendour and Porthglaze Coves, and approached Gurnard's Head, once an Iron Age settlement. I thought about the strange fish after which the headland is named, and imagined what the scene would look like if a fish (it would, of course, have to be a giant) replaced the headland. Thinking that the shandy might have got to me, I broke out of my reverie and continued to the climbing grounds around Bosigran.

The cliffs at Bosigran have some extremely difficult climbs.

On my way, I was able to look inland at the fascinating network of small fields lined with tall stone walls and hedges. These fields, dating back to the Bronze and Iron Ages, belong to a small farm of some 32 hectares (80 acres) near the ruined engine houses at Carn Galver. They have great heritage value, and most are managed as part of the Environmentally Sensitive Areas (ESA) Scheme.

An ESA is an area where the Department for Environment, Food and Rural Affairs (Defra) works with

The Climbers' Club at Bosigran, formerly a count house.

local farmers to conserve and protect particular local features. These may include wildlife as well as archaeological and historical monuments. Farmers in an ESA are encouraged to manage their land in an environmentally sensitive manner.

The cliffs around Bosigran have some spectacularly difficult climbs, where brave people test their skills and fortitude. During the Second World War, Commandos trained on one of the ridges on the western side of a valley; it is named 'Commando Ridge' in honour of their exploits.

*Two climbers on a ridge near Bosigran.**

In 1963, Lord Hunt, as Sir John Hunt, climbed the cliffs with Sherpa Tensing to celebrate their team's conquest of Everest ten years earlier. Apparently it was the first time that Tensing had ever climbed sea cliffs.

Today, many who climb here use the Climbers' Club hut (a former counting house) for overnight stays. Spectacular and exciting as the cliffs are, climbing them is not for the faint-hearted or the unskilled. They are very dangerous and should not be attempted without guidance from an expert.

On the way to Pendeen Watch I saw, silhouetted against the evening sky, two climbers on the knife-edge of a high ridge. I grew dizzy just looking at them. No novices these, they moved with apparent ease towards the summit, pausing occasionally to admire a view few others would have the skill or stomach to enjoy.

Many years ago, when I was leading a walk in the Lake District and was fit enough to set a fast pace, one of my companions, a climber and rock-climbing instructor, exclaimed that he would love to get me on the end of a rope. However, I never took up his kind offer to teach me the rudiments of climbing. Not equipped with the skills needed to scramble even the easier routes of Bosrigan, I continued on my pedestrian way to Portheras Cove, where I happened upon a contrasting scene. Sitting sedate and totally secure on the rocky slopes overlooking the cove, an amateur artist was painting the sea and coastline in the setting sun.

The lighthouse at Pendeen Watch was opened in 1900.

I chatted to the lady and discovered that she had come all the way from California to take part in an art class in the area.

When I left Portheras, I auto-piloted my way to Pendeen Watch, thinking that cliff walkers, climbers and artists appear very different, but each activity is driven by a similar passion for the raw natural beauty of the sea and the coast.

At Pendeen Watch, the lighthouse helps passing ships negotiate safely the dangerous waters around Gurnard's Head and Wra Rocks. Before the lighthouse was opened in 1900 many ships, unable to see either the Trevose or Longships lighthouses, met with disaster in these waters.

After admiring the lighthouse, I hobbled to the village of Pendeen and found the North Inn. Not only could I pitch my tent in its splendid campsite, but I could also have what the landlord unashamedly calls pub grub. The home-cooked steak and kidney pie with fresh vegetables, 'watered' down with a couple of pints was just the job after a long, gruelling scramble around the granite coastal tors of West Penwith.

Day 8 (15.6 ml/25.2 km)

Pendeen to Porthcurno

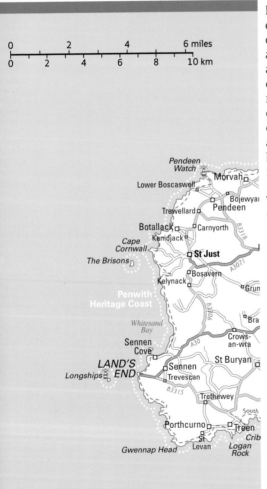

I had an excellent time at the Inn, eating, drinking, and enjoying the company. Pendeen itself is not really a holiday destination. It seems to be a vibrant village, with a community of Cornish people proud of their mining past and keen to share their cultural heritage with anyone interested. Geevor may be dead as an active mine, but it is still the means by which many Pendeen people make a living.

I left Pendeen at about 9.30 a.m. The plan was to meet Merryn at Cape Cornwall at noon; walk on to Porthcurno, and return to the North Inn where I had booked bed and breakfast for the two of us. I was able to leave my gear in the safe custody of the inn keeper. Unhampered, I seemed to float along, and soon rejoined the Coast Path just to the east of the lighthouse.

It was not until I returned home that I realized I'd missed the chance of looking at one of the most interesting features close to the Coast Path: the Iron Age fougou (underground chamber) behind Pendeen House. The house was once home to one Cornwall's great worthies, Dr William Borlase (1692–1772), who is regarded as the father of Cornish archaeology, and is one of my heroes. I knew when I started this

The headgear at Geevor Tin Mine.

Geevor Tin Mine: a World Heritage Site

Archaeological evidence indicates that miners have been at work around Geevor and Levant for at least 2,000 years. In the Bronze Age they extracted tin from metal-rich stones in streams. When these became less easy to find, solid rocks were dug out from veins on or near the surface. These early mining exploits could only take place above the water-table. It was not until water could be pumped out of mines that deep veins could be worked. This probably took place as early as the sixteenth century, but it was not until the early nineteenth century that steam-powered pumps allowed really deep mining to take place. The invention of dynamite made clearing rock a faster, if dangerous task. Shafts now reached depths of over 300 metres (1,000 feet).

From the nineteenth to the twentieth century, countless miles of underground shafts and galleries were dug, creating a labyrinth of dark passages. Some shafts at Levant Mine extend well below the sea bed where, it is said, miners could hear the rumble of massive boulders being shifted by ocean currents overhead.

Over the centuries, tin and copper provided a livelihood for many thousands of Cornish people. More than a few owners became incredibly rich. The cliff-top engine house at Levant lifted tin and copper to the surface for the last time in 1930, and Geevor finished commercial mining in 1990, but the mines and engine houses continue to provide an income for local people. Today, Geevor and Levant are World Heritage Sites, attracting visitors from all over the world. They come to Levant to see the beam engine steamed up especially for them; they visit Geevor to be guided through the workings by ex-miners, and to be told about the harsh realities of life above and below ground.

*The brilliantly coloured cliffs of Levant.**

project that it would be impossible for me to see everything, but this omission was disappointing. Never mind; it's another thing to look forward to doing sometime in the future.

Without realizing my loss, I headed for Cape Cornwall, taking one of the many paths eroded by the heavily booted tinners going to and from the mines on the sea cliffs. After only half a mile or so, I came face to face with one of the most spectacular scenes of the whole journey: the brilliantly coloured cliffs of Levant, ripped asunder by centuries of mining to reveal the blues, browns and reds of the minerals seeping out of their cut faces.

A path cut through the mine waste led me to the dramatically sited Levant Engine House. Now under the stewardship of the National Trust, it is staffed by members of the Trevithick Society, who have lovingly restored its beam engine, the oldest surviving one in England.

Levant mine was worked for 110 years. It covered half a mile (0.8 km) of coastline and ran about a quarter of a mile (0.4 km) inland. Its deepest shaft reached 350 fathoms (2,100 feet/640 metres). At first, miners had to use ladders to descend the shaft. This took so long that the Cornwall Polytechnic Society offered a prize for a speedy form of mechanical transport. The winner was Matthew Loam who, in 1841, invented a primitive lift mechanism called a man engine. It was designed to allow miners to step on or off at various depths. It worked successfully for many years, but on 20 October 1919 the lift mechanism collapsed, killing over 30 miners.

Mining in Levant continued until 1930, but it was never the same after the disaster.

I had time only to view the outside of the engine house, and to consider how appropriate it was that the flag of St Piran was flying.

The colourful cliffs and historic engine house were more than enough to satisfy my senses, but they were almost forgotten when I saw a group of five Cornish choughs poking about for food among

St Piran's flag flying at Levant Engine House.*

the scree of mine workings at Levant. This was my first sighting of the Cornish bird in the wild. I've seen them in captivity, but that could not compare with the excitement at being with these wonderful birds on the spectacular cliffs at Levant. In their natural habitat, they look much sleeker and more attractive than in captivity, and are quite unlike other crow species, which seem ugly in comparison.

The flag of St Piran flying at Levant Engine House

The origins and meaning of the famous flag are unknown (and much disputed). It was mentioned as being the banner of Cornwall in the first half of the nineteenth century, so it is likely to be much older. The claim that a group of Cornishmen carried it into the Battle of Agincourt is hard to prove, but an attractive idea. At about the same time, Cornwall's Breton neighbours apparently had a banner that showed a black cross on a white background, so perhaps the two flags have similar origins.

According to one legend, the cross represents the stream of molten tin found by St Piran on his blackened hearth when he rediscovered the skill of tin-smelting. It hardly seems likely, however, that the Cornish would need to rediscover a skill in use since the Bronze Age. Another theory is that it represents the lodes of tin lying in the dark ground. Yet another, that it represents good and evil.

However the flag came into being, and whatever the cross represents, it is now more widespread than ever. As well as being flown on special days, particularly St Piran's Day on 5 March, the cross is used as a symbol on everything from the Cornwall Library Service logo to Ginster's pasties. There was a brief moment of international fame when, presumably to the bemusement of many, Lisa Simpson waved St Piran's flag on a special Christmas edition of *The Simpsons*.

An amusing way to pass the time (at least in our nerdish household) when you are watching any large gathering on the television is to play a game of spot the flag. The last night of the proms, pop concerts and, in more recent years, protest marches in support of the countryside, are likely venues. There's usually a lone St Piran's cross being waved somewhere in the crowd.

The Cornish chough
(Pyrrhocorax pyrrhocorax)
The chough is easily distinguished from other members of the crow family by its bright red bill and red legs. It is unique among crows in being a specialist feeder. It uses its long curved bill to probe maritime turf, ant hills and animal dung for ants, beetles, fly larvae, worms and other invertebrates.

The chough is not exclusively Cornish, but this enigmatic and attractive bird was so strongly associated with Cornwall that it became the county's emblem, featuring prominently on its coat of arms.

In former times, the chough was very common on Cornwall's coast, breeding mainly in crevices or holes in sea caves. But in 1947 it ceased to breed, and by 1973 it was officially regarded as extinct in the county. When this happened, many people felt greatly saddened by the loss of an integral part of Cornwall's identity.

A project entitled Operation Chough was launched in 1987, with the aim of re-introducing choughs from individuals bred in captivity. In the foreword to a booklet published to mark the launch, Prince Charles, Duke of Cornwall, wrote: 'If the Chough can return to Cornwall, and therefore England too, it would be of great symbolic importance and pride to Cornish people and all those concerned with wildlife conservation.'

Although Operation Chough was unsuccessful in its attempts to reintroduce the chough, and despite many supporters believing that it would never return unaided, wild choughs have made their own way back to Cornwall to breed.

The chough is fully protected, including its nest and eggs. It is illegal to disturb it for the purpose of photography or any other reason, except under licence. For the benefit of chough-loving visitors to West Cornwall, in the summer of 2007, closed-circuit television cameras were set up under licence so that nesting adults and their young chicks could be seen with minimum disturbance.

From Levant I continued towards Porthledden Cove and Cape Cornwall. I was so absorbed in thoughts of choughs that I barely noticed the two engine houses by the inclined Crowns shaft of Botallack. Their spectacular position on the side of the cliff make these probably the most photographed engine houses in Cornwall, if not the world.

The Botallack mine yielded mainly copper, but tin and iron were also obtained. Like the Levant mine, the workings of Botallack stretched under the sea. Wilkie Collins, the famous Victorian author, went down the mine in 1851, and wrote a very vivid description of his experiences in his book *Rambles Beyond Railways*.

Soon after passing Botallack Head, I entered Kenidjack, another area of world significance, both historically and archaeologically. As well as having an Iron Age castle with well-defined bank-and-ditch defences on its steep-sided promontory, it also has a wealth of remnants left over the centuries by the exploits of countless Cornish tinners.

Surface workings date back to medieval times. The ruins of water-wheels and engine houses, and the dried-up channels of leats are the

Wilkie Collins and Botallack mine

The following is from Wilkie Collins' account in *Rambles Beyond Railways* of his experiences of going down Botallack Mine with a miner-guide via a series of perpendicular ladders:

> ... four hundred yards out, under the bottom of the sea; and twenty fathoms or a hundred and twenty feet below the sea level... and there are galleries deeper yet, even below that!

> After listening for a few moments, a distant, unearthly noise becomes faintly audible – a long, low, mysterious moaning, which never changes, which is felt on the ear as well as heard by it – a sound that might proceed from some incalculable distance, from some invisible height – a sound so unlike anything that is heard on the upper ground, in the free air of heaven; so sublimely mournful and still; and so ghostly and impressive when listened to in the subterranean recesses of the earth, that we continue instinctively to hold our peace, as if enchanted by it, and think not of communicating to each other the awe and astonishment which it has inspired in us from the very first.

> At last, the miner speaks again, and tells us that what we hear is the sound of the surf lashing the rocks a hundred and twenty feet above us, and of the waves that are breaking on the beach beyond... when storms are at their height, when the ocean hurls mountain after mountain of water on the cliffs, then the noise is terrific; the roaring heard down here in the mine is so expressively fierce and awful, that the boldest men at work are afraid to continue their labour. All ascend to the surface, to breathe the upper air and stand on the firm earth...

remains of intense mining activity that took place in the eighteenth and nineteenth centuries. (Leats are narrow channels ingeniously engineered to carry water by the force of gravity alone, from the river and reservoirs high in the valley to the many mining sites lower down.)

Tregaseal River was really nothing much more than a stream, but it was vital to Victorian mining. Its water was used to drive about 50 waterwheels, and in the processing of minerals. It was reported at the time that the River entered the mining area crystal clear, but left stained the colour of blood.

When I reached Porthledden Cove, I crossed its valley and walked out to Cape Cornwall.

I rendezvoused with Merryn an hour later than planned. While I was enjoying the splendours of West Penwith, she had the unpleasant and potentially dangerous experience of a tyre blow-out on the A30. Thankfully, no one was hurt nor any serious damage done and, after a tyre change, she was able complete her journey.

After sharing lunch and exchanging stories of the morning's happenings, we left to make our separate ways to Porthcurno. Merryn was taking the car there so that we could return to Pendeen together; I was walking to complete a few more miles of my journey.

I followed the tracks below Cape Cornwall golf course up to Carn Gloose (or Carn Gluze as some people spell it). Just off the Coast Path is

Cape Cornwall, gifted to the nation in 1987.*

Cape Cornwall

This is the only cape in Britain. Geographically, a cape is the point at which two seas meet. Cape Cornwall gained its title from the mistaken belief that it is the point at which the St George's Channel meets the English Channel. Experts now think that Gwennap Head near Land's End is more deserving of the title, but the precise boundary between the two seas is not static, and shifts from time to time.

Like most promontories, Cape Cornwall was the site of an ancient cliff castle. Today its most prominent feature is its tall chimney stack. Once linked via a long flue to a whim (winding) engine house, the chimney failed to fulfil its primary purpose because it could not produce a sufficient draught. Nevertheless, it was retained as a navigation aid and has carried out its secondary function well.

In 1987, the Cape was gifted to the nation by H.J. Heinz Ltd., and placed in the care of the National Trust to mark the Heinz Company's centenary. The Cape had previously been owned by Francis Oates who, in 1860, at the age of 12 worked in a mine near St Just. He emigrated to South Africa, and made his fortune. He bought Cape Cornwall at the beginning of the twentieth century, and died in 1918.

Bollowal Barrow.

Bollowall Barrow. With its dramatic cliff-top setting, it is regarded by many as the most spectacularly sited and most outstanding funereal site in Cornwall. Until 1878, when W. Copeland Borlase (a descendant of my hero William Borlase) excavated it, it had lain hidden for decades under tons of waste from the St Just United Mine. The complex stone chambers date from the Early to Middle Bronze Age (2500–1500 BC); they were probably built by the local community as a shrine or tomb for the dead.

The raised beach at Porth Nanven.

I continued along the Coast Path from Carn Gloose down Cot Valley to the beach of Porth Nanven. This beach has been nicknamed Dinosaur Egg Beach because of its large, ovoid boulders.

Porth Nanven: Dinosaur Egg Beach

Porth Nanven is an area of SSI, mainly because of its geological features. The most fantastic are the ultra-smooth, ovoid boulders strewn across the shore and embedded in the cliff at the back of the beach. They come in all sizes, from a few centimetres (the size of hens' eggs) to a metre or more in length (the size of fossilized dinosaur eggs). They are so attractive that in the past many were taken to be used as ornaments. A city in the north of England used a large number of 'dinosaur eggs' from Porth Nanven in its city-centre displays. It is now illegal to remove any stones or boulders from the beach.

The boulders on the beach and in the cliff immediately behind it acquired their smooth surfaces by being bashed against each other in violent seas about 120,000 years ago.

Despite recent sea-level rises, the present high-tide mark at Porth Nanven is much lower than it was 120,000 years ago. An upward tilting of the land, following the removal of ice caps from northern Britain during the post-glacial period, resulted in ancient marine material being left high and dry. This formed the raised beach that is now the cliff immediately above the present high-tide mark.

Storms and other forces have exposed the vertical face of the raised beach, revealing wave-worn boulders and pebbles in a matrix of mud and sand. Although it's tempting to take a close look, be warned. Giant boulders may break away at any time to join others on the shore, making the vertical face of the raised beach unsafe to approach without great care.

The slipway at Sennen Cove.

A fisherman and his dog check his boat at Sennen Cove.

When I'd finished examining the 'dinosaur eggs' at Porth Nanven, I zig-zagged my way up the Coast Path to Gribba Point, and then went along the top of the cliffs that lead to Whitesand Bay and Sennen Cove.

Sennen Cove, lying between the headlands of Land's End and Cape Cornwall, has been referred to as 'a veritable haven amongst these jaws of death'. In the nineteenth century, as in most other coastal places, fishing dominated the lives of local people. It was during this time that they cleared boulders from the shore, so they could haul their boats up the beach. The boulders were used to create the protective sea wall called The Back. How things have changed. Sennen Cove still has a number of active fishermen, but life is dominated by tourism.

I didn't stop long at Sennen Cove; the beach and shops were very crowded, and there was not much to see on the slipway or jetty as most of the half-dozen or so Sennen-based fishing boats were out at sea. The fishermen work their nets, pots and handlines between spring and autumn.

Land's End and Longships lighthouse.*

When I returned in November it was quite different, and probably more reminiscent of Sennen's past. There were few people about, but the jetty was crammed high with pots and nets from boats being laid up for the winter. Crabs and lobsters tend to move into deeper water in winter and, because the water is much colder, they are less inclined to take bait. In any case, the days are far too short, and the inshore waters around Land's End are far too treacherous and unpredictable to fish in winter.

Land's End often marks the beginning or end of long-distance walks, but was approximately half-way in my journey. I was just over eight days into what was to be a 16-day walk.

Many first-time visitors are disappointed to find that Land's End is not the grandest place on the Cornish coast. Its status as a major tourist attraction is a result of the land here projecting a little further westwards than its fellow headlands. Nevertheless, it has great symbolic significance as the place where Cornwall stops and the rest of the world begins.

Like many others who have come to the towering cliff top to look westward over the apparently endless sea, my mind turned to thoughts of the infinite. I recalled the words of Folliott-Stokes when he paused to ponder at Land's End: 'Another thousand years,' we say to ourselves, 'and what manner of ships will be passing? Who will be sitting here? What will be their thoughts? And where shall we be?' Ah, that is the question.

Land's End is a major destination for holidaymakers, with many attractions in its tourist complex. One of these is *Return to the Last Labyrinth*,

The Armed Knight and Enys Dodnan off Land's End. *

but I was not tempted to 'thrill to tales of monsters, pirates, smugglers and wreckers', nor did I want to 'meet the great King Arthur and his brave knights, brought to life with stunning special effects', so I hurriedly left Land's End and turned south-east towards Porthcurno. It took me only 20 minutes or so to escape the tourist flocks and reach the rugged solitude of Pordenack Point, passing the Armed Knight and Enys Dodnan on the way. The lichen-covered, flower-topped, castellated pinnacles of Pordenack Point are superb. No wonder the artist Turner was so inspired by them that he tried to capture their majestic beauty in a drawing.

It never ceases to amaze me that if you are prepared to walk just a short distance from car-parks, even in the height of summer, you can have the glories of the Coast Path more or less to yourself. An occasional encounter with a fellow walker, and a quick exchange of pleasantries enhances rather than detracts from the experience. But I saw no one until I reached Nanjizal Bay.

As I continued on my way around the Bay, I was haunted by a peculiar and very deep sound. This was not the call of a love-sick mermaid, nor some sea monster, but came from a buoy about a mile offshore, between Tol-Pedn-Penwith and Hella Point. The constant moans warn of the Run-

Porthgwarra, with its granite slipway, fisherman's passage and storage caves.

nel Stone – a treacherous rock just below the surface of the sea. In 1923, the steamer *City of Westminster* collided with the rock with such force that it decapitated it, removing the top six metres (20 feet) or so. Even decapitated, the Runnel Stone is still lethal.

On the top of the cliff are land markers – one red, the other black and white – that also help mariners to avoid the Runnel Stone. If sailing just off shore, the trick is to keep the black-and-white marker in sight; if it becomes blocked by the red marker, it is probably too late to save your vessel from being holed.

The whole stretch of coast between the Longships lighthouse and Gwennap Head is notoriously hazardous for shipping. It is where opposing tidal currents collide – the English Channel coming from the east, and the St George's Channel from the west. This collision, when combined with strong winds and thick fog, tests the competence of even experienced mariners. In stormy conditions, when winds can suddenly veer from north-westerly to south-westerly, the sea is thrown into total confusion. It's no wonder that mariners call this The Throes or that its choppy seas are, for obvious reasons, referred to as the 'pooks'. If a reminder is needed of how dangerous this area is, then just think of the more than

Porthgwarra

The most striking feature of Porthgwarra is the stone-paved tunnel going through the cliff (page 93). Originally, there were two separate passages, one above the other.

According to Folliott-Stokes, they were hand-drilled by St Just miners in the 1890s, to allow boats to be taken to a higher level. Another source suggests that the passages were drilled to provide farmers with easier access to the beach for seaweed.

In 1996, the rock separating them collapsed, forming the single opening seen today.

When Folliott-Stokes visited Porthgwarra at the beginning of the twentieth century, he thought it would be an ideal smuggler's cove. At the top of the beach, above a rusty old capstan, are two man-made caves (above). Although empty when I entered them, they look just the kind of place where nineteenth-century smugglers might have stored contraband. In *The Cornish Coast and Moors*, Folliott-Stokes wrote:

> No one could possibly have lived here in olden days and not smuggled. As we pass the corner of a whitewashed, thatch-roofed cabin, with a great chimney and a huge boulder built into one of its ends, we think of the stories those old walls could tell of contraband, of desperate ventures and cunning artifices, of golden spoil and brimming beakers of the red wine of France. The good old days never to return. Days of action and adventure, when risks were daily taken and thought nothing of.

Perhaps the two man-made caves that I found empty once hid smuggled goods.

130 recorded wrecks, and probably countless others, lying on the sea bed between Gwennap Head and Gurnard's Head.

Approaching Gwennap Head, I forgot the instructions in *The South West Coast Path Guide* that 'Care should be taken to keep to the seaward path out to Gwennap Head', and mistakenly took the inland path. Although this was easier, I missed the natural arch at Tol-Pedn-Penwith ('the holed headland of Penwith'), and other grand sights. Yet another place to add to my 'still to do' list.

Although I failed to see the full glory of Gwennap Head, I did drop down into Porthgwarra, and took a good look at its granite slipway, fisherman's passage and storage caves.

I left Porthgwarra along the track in front of its still whitewashed cottages, and followed it up to Carn Barges. Then I descended to Porth Chapel, stopping to have a look at St Levan's Holy Well on the way. The well is located on the footpath, and overlooks the beach. It is protected by a wall and has two slabs capping it. Water can be seen only in one corner.

St Levan's Holy Well, on the footpath to Porth Chapel.

I didn't go on to the beach, but climbed towards the headland of Pedn-men-an-mere. From there, it was but a short walk to the car-park behind the Minack Theatre. I found the path parallel to and behind the Theatre entrance; paused to admire the spectacular view of Porthcurno, and then descended the steep steps to rejoin Merryn on the beach.

From Porthcurno, we drove back to Pendeen to spend the night in the comfort of a chalet behind the North Inn.

Minack Theatre

This fabulously sited theatre hewn from rock on the steep cliffs overlooking Porthcurno beach was planned, built and financed by Rowena Cade. Born in Derbyshire in 1893, she came to Cornwall in the 1920s, and bought the Minack Headland. Rowena built Minack House for herself and her family, and became involved in local theatre productions. In 1930 her garden was suggested as the ideal location for a production of *The Tempest*, but it was too small. So Rowena, working with two local craftsmen, extended the garden out into the gully above Minack Rock and made a small outdoor theatre there. After much hard work, *The Tempest* was performed in 1932. Its setting, overlooking a rugged coastline and tempestuous sea, was so appropriate and well-received that it prompted a report in *The Times*. This inspired Rowena Cade to improve and extend the Theatre. Since then, hundreds of plays and musicals have been performed at the Minack. Among the most frequent and the most popular has been *The Pirates of Penzance*. In 1976, when she was well over 80, Rowena Cade gave the Theatre to a charitable trust, The Minack Theatre Trust, which manages it today.

Porthcurno to Marazion

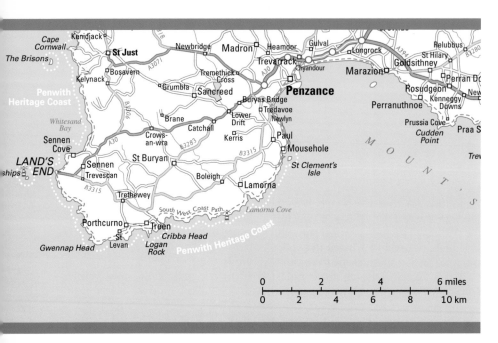

It was a wet, grim day. Reluctant to leave the comfort of the North Inn, we had a leisurely breakfast, packed and prevaricated. Then Merryn drove me to the car-park just below the Museum of Submarine Telegraphy at Porthcurno where she was to abandon me, once again, to my fate.

Over dinner the previous evening, Merryn had told me about the museum, which she had been able to go around while waiting for me. It sounded as if it would be well worth a visit. But I had time only to look at the small building just above the beach and the outside of the museum before starting the ninth day of my walk.

At the back of Porthcurno beach, I used a short path to take me round the next headland. The path passes behind the earthworks at Treryn Dinas. As it was wet and visibility was poor, I decided to postpone a diversion out to the headland until another day, and continued on to Penberth Cove.

Porthcurno beach, looking towards Treryn Dinas.

Porthcurno Telegraph Museum

This is a jewel of a museum, and well worth the short diversion for the pleasure of visiting it. It has a treasure trove of information about the work at Porthcurno when it was a cable station, exhibits both technical and quirky, as well as an interesting local history of the area.

The museum is run by very pleasant, helpful and knowledgeable staff and volunteers, some of whom used to work for the Cable & Wireless Company. They are proud of the atmosphere within the museum, and rightly so. There is a very good balance between the educational and the entertaining. Who would have thought the history of cable-laying and submarine telegraphy could be made so interesting? Children are not forgotten, and there are lots of hands-on activities designed for them. This museum has not made the mistake of relying too heavily on new technology to keep youngsters (and adults) amused. Instead, there is a good mix, with emphasis on puzzles and activities rather than computer screens.

One of the attractions of the museum is the building itself, which is largely underground. Work had been carried out at Porthcurno since 1870 when the British end of the first undersea cable (from Bombay) came ashore there. In 1940, the threat of attack led to the work moving underground. Local tin miners created two tunnels where the work could be carried out. They also cut out of solid granite a set of 120 stairs at the back of the tunnels, so the workers could escape should the worst happen. Now visitors to the museum can climb those same stairs to a viewing platform on the cliffs.

Sadly, work as a cable station at Porthcurno came to an end in 1970, 100 years after it began. For a while, it was kept on by Cable & Wireless as a training college, but it finally closed in 1993, when training was transferred to Coventry, opening again four years later as a museum. The museum and staff maintain connection with the parent company, however, and volunteers at the museum still use the old workshop to repair and maintain equipment in the exhibits.

Returning to Treryn Dinas on a sunny day in November, I was able to explore the magnificent granite headland, make the steep climb to its exposed summit, and admire the nearby coves in all their glowing glory. I felt like Folliott-Stokes when he scampered to the top of the headland and was inspired to write 'what an eyrie for a poet! and even to the average man what a dream-compelling spot is the topmost tower of this old sea-girt fighting-place!' (from *The Cornish Coast and Moors*). His description of the coves he saw from there could have been written today:

> They are, where the rock is granite or basaltic, guarded by cliffs and headlands crowned with pinnacles which give them the appearance of titanic castles. The sides of these natural bastions glow with many-coloured lichens.... These secluded amphitheatres of stern grandeur and vivid beauty enclose water so deeply blue that one can only liken it to melted sapphire, save when it approaches the little scimitar of sand at the foot of the cliffs; then it becomes the purest emerald green...

While at Treryn Dinas, I managed to get close to its Logan Rock. But unlike a previous visitor, I made no attempt to dislodge it.

The Logan Rock at Treryn Dinas

Treryn Dinas means 'fortress settlement', but the headland is famed not so much for being the site of an Iron Age cliff castle, as for having a particularly interesting logan rock. Logan rocks are delicately balanced rocking stones that acquired their precarious nature from horizontal weathering of granite outcrops. The Logan Rock at Treryn Dinas, though well known, is not the easiest to rock, but the reason for this is the reason for its fame.

In 1824 the Logan Stone was so finely balanced that one person, acting alone, could rock it. In that year, a lieutenant in the Royal Navy decided to disprove the theory that the stone, though easily moved, could not be displaced. He and some of his crew set to work with levers and managed to dislodge it, tumbling the stone over the edge of the cliff. By good fortune, instead of falling into the sea, the stone was caught in a crevice.

This act of vandalism was spotted by local workmen, who reported it to the landowner, and he was furious. There was widespread anger in the area, partly against the presumption of a stranger having the nerve to move a significant local landmark, and one of geographical interest, but also because the stone had been a great tourist attraction. The locals had been making money out of it, and this source of income was almost certain to dry up. The Admiralty, realizing that this was bad public relations for them, and no doubt influenced by the anger of an important local landowner, told the unfortunate lieutenant to put the stone back into its original place. He would be allowed to use all the material resources of the local dockyards, but any expense of labour would have to be paid for out of his own purse.

It took months of effort with pulleys, chains, capstans and human labour, but finally, in November 1824, the stone was replaced. Unfortunately, it was not positioned correctly, and since then the stone has not moved with the same ease as before.

Long-liners and potters still operate from Penberth Cove.

As I descended the path to Penberth Cove, I could see why this delightful spot is so often photographed and painted. Though small, it is beautiful, and there are so many things to look at: the large capstan, dating from before 1840, and beautifully restored by the National Trust; the remains of the pilchard presses in the fish cellar (called the 'Big Cellar'), and the slipway with its rounded stones polished by many years' use, all indicate that Penberth Cove was once a thriving fishing village. Although catches are much smaller than they used to be, up to ten small long-liners and potters still operate from the cove today.

I crossed the slipway; looked at the fascinating stone clapper bridge nearby, and climbed up the cove side to the cliff top to continue walking eastward. After passing behind the automated lighthouse at Tater-Du, I entered a scrubby, granite landscape. Just off the Coast Path I came across a rickety wooden gate which marked the entry to an unexpected treat – the Minack Chronicles Nature Reserve, created by Derek and Jeannie Tangye.

The Tangyes had come to Cornwall in 1950 to grow daffodils, early potatoes and other crops as tenants of Dorminack, a nearby flower farm. They had both had successful careers in London, but wanted to escape the city to live a rural life.

The entrance to the Tangyes' nature reserve.

The Minack Chronicles Nature Reserve

During his time in Cornwall, Derek Tangye wrote an evocative and sometimes philosophical account of his life in West Penwith, in a series of books known as the Minack Chronicles. They became hugely popular with readers who wanted to share, however vicariously, his life of quiet contemplation and self-discovery in what was then a remote part of England.

In 1976, Derek and Jeannie acquired 8 hectares (20 acres) of land near Dorminack. They left this land 'wild and untamed' to attract animals and plants. One of the animals it attracted was Oliver, a black cat which came to live with the Tangyes and featured in the Chronicles. The Minack Chronicles Trust was formed to protect the land, which became known as Oliver Land, or the Minack Chronicles Nature Reserve.

Today, this private reserve is managed much as the Tangyes would have wished, as 'a place for solitude'. Most of it is relatively untouched, and appears unkempt, but it attracts many animals. Among them are badgers, foxes, lizards, frogs, kestrels, buzzards, and black cap, and the red admiral butterfly that feeds on the nectar of the creeping thistle, one of the many plants in the Reserve.

The Merry Maidens

The Merry Maidens is a circle of 19 stones, 23 metres (75 feet) in diameter, dating from the Bronze Age. Its near perfect symmetry makes it one of the most famous and most visited megalithic sites in Britain. According to legend, the stones are the petrified bodies of 19 maidens who dared to dance on the Sabbath. The Pipers – two tall stones in a nearby field – are what's left of the guilty musicians. Archaeologists believe the circle was constructed for some religious or ritual purpose, but do not know exactly what. Today, the circle is one of the places where the Cornish Gorsedd ceremony is held. This is the annual meeting at which new bards are admitted to the Gorsedd, or College of Bards – an organization unique to Celtic communities, designed to perpetuate their cultural heritage.

Another place worth visiting is the Merry Maidens, about a half mile or so inland from the Nature Reserve.

Back on the Coast Path, the track down to Lamorna Cove is quite different from the exposed and wind-pruned coastal paths around Land's End: it is sheltered, and overgrown with lush vegetation. The drizzly conditions made the vegetation very wet, and my clothing became soaked. But at least it was not actually raining.

The woods of the river valley extend almost down to the shore, making Lamorna Cove very attractive to artists and photographers. Its small quay was built to ship granite from the quarry cut into the cliffs leading up to Carn Du.

In the nineteenth century, the granite blocks were much sought after. Many were used in the building of the Thames Embankment, and one was used to create a 7-metre (22-feet) high obelisk which featured in the Great Exhibition at Crystal Palace in 1851.

As I walked the remaining few miles to Mousehole, I encountered

Monterey pine was planted at Kemyel Crease to act as a windbreak. *

a plantation of Monterey pine at Kemyel Crease. The once terraced and cultivated slopes were purchased by the Cornwall Wildlife Trust in 1974.

Monterey pine (*Pinus radiata*), a native of a few locations on the Pacific coast of California, had been planted at Kemyel Crease to provide a windbreak. Its height (up to 60 metres/200 feet when cultivated and cared for in ideal conditions), its year-round leaf cover, and its bold shape make it

Lamorna Cove used to ship granite. *

an effective one. It is also attractive because of its highly fissured bark, which varies in colour from grey to brown, and the clusters of large cones that may remain on its branches for many years.

The tall conifers give the sloping granite cliffs a distinctly exotic appearance. Growing head and shoulders above the other cliff-side trees, the Monterey pine can be seen from miles offshore, making them a useful landmark for passing vessels.

Apart from conserving the pine, the CWT has encouraged the growth of broad-leaved trees. Together with the pine, they have made the reserve a haven for wildlife on the otherwise windswept cliffs.

Mousehole – 'the loveliest village in England'.

I entered Mousehole by the very steep Raginnis Hill. Dylan Thomas, the poet and author of *Under Milkwood*, frequently came here, and called this hill 'Raginnis-is-good-for-you Hill'. Thomas also referred to Mousehole as 'The loveliest village in England'.

Although it looks serene today, Mousehole's history is not all peace and calm. On 23 July 1595, four Spanish men-of-war anchored on what was subsequently called Spaniard Point. They raided the village, and sacked it. Then they marched up the hill to burn Paul Church, before moving on to ransack Newlyn and Penzance.

In Mousehole only one building, the Keigwyn Arms, escaped the torch. Even so, its owner, Jenkin Keigwyn, is reputed to have been killed by a Spanish cannonball. Keigwyn House, as it is now called, was built around the fourteenth century. It still stands, the oldest building in the village.

I had not visited Mousehole since childhood, and I found it an absolute delight. It was fascinating to walk its narrow streets and see the links to its distant Elizabethan past, and its not-so-distant days as an important fishing port. I was not long in Mousehole before window displays in shops such as the Cat and Mouse reminded me that Mousehole is also known for the legend of Tom Bawcock.

Mousehole is famous around Christmas not only for Tom Bawcock's Eve, but also for its Christmas lights. Displays are set up all round the village, and around and in the harbour.

I was so taken with Mousehole that I returned twice after my walk. The first time was in November when I saw the Christmas lights being installed. The second was in December,

A shop window in Mousehole. three days after the lights had been turned on.

Restaurants, shops and galleries were open, and roasted chestnuts were being sold on the harbourside. I was one of many people who came from far and wide to Mousehole and thoroughly enjoyed the festivities.

Back in June, I left Mousehole along the road that follows the coast in front of Penlee Quarry to Newlyn. An alternative route is up the hill through the small village of Paul, to reach Newlyn from behind the Quarry. The first route has the advantage of a sea view; the second allows you to visit Paul churchyard, where Dolly Pentreath is buried.

The legend of Tom Bawcock

Towards one Christmas, the exact date long forgotten, Mousehole was in grave danger. For some time storms had prevented boats going out to sea. Without any fish to eat, villagers were slowly starving to death. That is until one local fisherman, Tom Bawcock, braved the heavy seas to bring back a bumper catch and save them all. To celebrate this daring deed, the people of Mousehole have a special festival on 23 December, called Tom Bawcock's Eve. The main event of the evening is the procession through the village of a huge Starry Gazey Pie (a pie of many fishes, with the heads sticking up through the pastry, 'star-gazing') – a reminder of the fish feast that Tom Bawcock provided. The exploits of Tom Bawcock have become famous far beyond Mousehole, partly through *The Mousehole Cat*, a children's book by author Antonia Barber and illustrator Nicola Bayley, which retells the tale of Tom Bawcock through the eyes of Mowser, his cat.

Dolly Pentreath, mentioned in connection with John Davey's memorial stone at Zennor church (page 77), is reputed to have been the last speaker of the ancient Cornish language. She was a fishwife, regularly walking long distances to sell catches. No doubt this was a very hard living, but it must have been quite healthy as she died in 1777 at the ripe old age of 102.

On my way to Newlyn, I stopped at the Penlee Lifeboat Disaster Memorial Gardens to pay my respects to the men who sacrificed their lives in their attempt to save others.

The Penlee lifeboat disaster

It was on 19 December 1981 that disaster struck. The coaster *Union Star* had developed an engine fault in atrocious weather. Winds gusting to force 12 (95 mph) made the seas heavy and treacherous. The *Union Star* was pushed on to the rocks at Boscawen Cove, near Lamorna.

Conditions were so bad that a helicopter from RNAS Culdrose could not remove any of the five crew or three passengers. The 47-foot (14-metre) Penlee Lifeboat *Solomon Browne* was called out, with Coxswain Trevelyan Richards in charge. It was crewed by eight experienced seamen, all from Mousehole. Conditions were so dangerous that only one man from each family was allowed in the crew.

Facing waves over 15 metres (50 feet) high, the lifeboat went head on into the stormy seas and retrieved four of the eight on board the *Union Star*. Although the *Solomon Browne* was forced away from the stricken vessel, she went back to rescue those remaining on board. The last message heard from the lifeboat's radio was 'We've got four of them off, hang on, we have got four at the moment. There's two left on board...' . No more was heard from the lifeboat and, after her lights disappeared, no more was seen of her either. Lifeboats from Sennen Cove, the Lizard and even St Mary's, Isles of Scilly, tried to search and rescue. But to no avail. All 16 lives from the two boats were lost; only eight bodies were ever found – four from the *Solomon Browne*, and four from the *Union Star*.

Trevelyan Richards was awarded the Royal National Lifeboat Institution's Gold Medal, and the rest of the crew were all awarded Bronze Medals, all posthumously.

Every year on 19 December, the Mousehole Christmas lights are turned off at 8 p.m. for one hour in remembrance of the gallant crew.

Inscribed on a board in the Penlee Disaster Memorial Gardens, close to the names of the lost crew, is the following stirring description of a lifeboat, made by Sir Winston Churchill:

> It drives on with a mercy which does not quail in the presence of death.
> It drives on as a proof, a symbol, a testimony that man is created in the image of God and that valour and virtue have not perished in the British race.

The bravery of the men on the *Solomon Browne* remains an inspiration to those who crew its replacement, a modern Severn class lifeboat and an inshore Atlantic 75 class lifeboat. Both are stationed in Newlyn.

The RNMDSF, Newlyn.

In Newlyn, I visited two buildings: the Royal National Mission to Deep Sea Fishermen (RNMDSF), in which I enjoyed the best home-made chips (served with a perfectly cooked egg) that I have ever had, and the Newlyn Art Gallery, in which I saw a grand exhibition of local artwork.

Bloated by my excellent lunch, I sauntered along the North Pier to look at the boats in the harbour, and the lighthouse at the end of the South Pier opposite. Newlyn is the

Newlyn harbour.

most active fishing port in Cornwall, and a wide range of fish is sold in the fish market.

The lighthouse is not only a beacon for boats. Attached to it and rising above its light are a weather vane, and the antenna of a very special global positioning system (GPS). The GPS is linked to a tidal gauge located in the sea below the Ordnance Tidal Observatory, a few metres away from the lighthouse. A brass bolt in the Tidal Observatory acts as the UK Fundamental Benchmark, from which all tidal data in

The Penlee Severn Class lifeboat,
Ivan Ellen, *in Newlyn harbour.*

tide tables and Ordnance Survey maps are referenced. Using this benchmark and continuous recordings made by the nearby tide gauge and the GPS, scientists are able to monitor sea-level rises and provide objective information vital to studies of global warming.

I went back along the North Pier to the main road, turned right and made my way to the Newlyn Art Gallery. The gallery was opened over 100 years ago, to promote local artwork. Unlike many galleries, it was established by artists, not architects. These artists had come to Newlyn to paint outdoors, in the open-air style known as *plein air*. The group became known as the Newlyn School after the success in 1885 at the

Cornish Catch, *by Susie Ray, shows some of the many fish caught off the coast of Cornwall by Newlyn fishermen. These include baleen wrasse, mackerel, cuckoo wrasse, dogfish, pollack, garfish, red gurnard, weever fish, cod, and John Dory.*

The Promenade, Penzance.

Royal Academy of *A Fish Sale on a Cornish Beach*, a painting by Stanhope Forbes. Because of his great influence, Stanhope Forbes is regarded as the founder of the Newlyn School. A bust the great man adorns the outside wall of the Gallery, which now delivers nationally significant exhibitions and educational projects. Amazingly, entry is free.

From the gallery, I walked along the promenade to Penzance, and diverted into the town to look at the Egyptian House and the Humphry Davy statue.

The Egyptian House

With its sphinx-like adornments, lotus columns and Royal Coat of Arms of George III and William IV, the Egyptian House in Chapel Street is the most flamboyant building in Penzance. It was designed in 1835 by a Plymouth architect, John Foulston, for a mineralogist, John Lavin, as a museum and repository of geological specimens. Its façade is thought to be a copy of that of a museum in Piccadilly, which itself was inspired by the Temple of Hathor in Dendera, Egypt. The style flourished after Napoleon's conquest of Egypt in 1798.

In the 1960s the building fell into partial disrepair. It is now owned by the Landmark Trust, which, in 1973, painstakingly restored it to its former glory.

Sir Humphry Davy

Cornwall does not have a habit of erecting statues, but Penzance made an exception for its most famous son, Humphry Davy (1778–1829). His impressive statue can be seen looking down on Market Jew Street (the name comes from a corruption of *Marghas Yaw*, the Cornish for Thursday Market). This is the street in which the young Davy is reputed to have stood on a cart telling Cornish folk-stories to crowds of children.

As an adult, Davy became interested in chemistry, gaining the title of Professor at the early age of 24. Among the long list of Davy's achievements are the application of nitrous oxide (laughing gas) as an anaesthetic used by dentists, and the discovery of a number of chemical elements. His most notable achievement was the invention of the miner's safety lamp, which provided light without the risk of lethal gas explosions. This invention alone probably saved thousands of lives all over the world, and it is appropriate that in his statue, Sir Humphry Davy holds one of his safety lamps in his right hand.

St Michael's Mount, Marazion. *

By the time I had seen the Egyptian House and sat at the feet of Sir Humphry Day, it was getting late and I was keen to find a campsite for the night. I left Penzance along the main road. Then I crossed the footbridge leading to the back of the beach and continued along the Coast Path in the direction of Marazion.

The miserable drizzle had cleared, and it was turning into a very pleasant sunny summer's evening. For the final part of the day's walk I was able to admire St Michael's Mount, as if it were a sculpture, from slightly different angles, and watch how the changing light highlighted different features of this jewel in Cornwall's seascape.

I reached Marazion at about 7 p.m. and, as previously arranged, I met Alison (Alison Hodge, the publisher of this book) at the hotel. Despite my weather-worn and unkempt appearance, they let me in, and Alison and I enjoyed a cup or two of coffee and chatted.

I was then left to find a place for the night. Heading towards the nearest campsite, I bumped into a friend and former colleague, Colin Pringle, and his wife Katie. I explained to them why I was in Marazion looking so dishevelled and apparently homeless and, without hesitation, they invited me to spend the night with them only a few yards up the road. An evening in such hospitable company was an unexpected bonus, and one of the highlights of my journey.

Marazion to Mullion

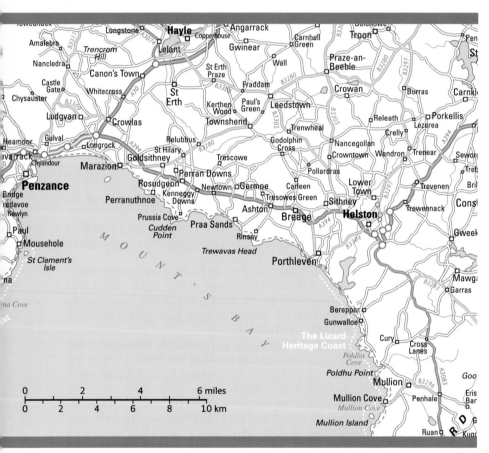

Before setting out on the tenth day of my walk, I had a wonderful break-fast of homemade grapefruit marmalade on toast made from freshly baked bread. After saying my farewells to Colin and Katie, I left Marazion and the former Benedictine monastery of St Michael's Mount, rejoined the Coast Path and plodded slowly through little fields to Cudden Point.

With muscles stiff and one of my toes badly blistered from all the walking, it took me almost two hours to get to Cudden Point. I decided to relieve the pressure on the blister by cutting away a piece of skin from the offending toe. The dead skin had become hardened to the consistency of tough leather by continual pounding. Using all the skills I developed through years of teaching biology practicals, I managed to dissect away the skin without causing myself serious injury. After this operation, I was able to walk with much less pain and my pace increased.

The path goes inland from the Point to Perranuthnoe (usually known simply as Perran), and from there to Prussia Cove, famous for its eighteenth-century smuggling activities.

From Prussia Cove, I walked to Praa Sands, had an egg sandwich and some fruit, and went quickly to Porthleven along the cliff top. This stretch of coast is dramatic and beautiful, but although I saw several engine houses on the way, the only thing that stopped me in my tracks was a bank of foxgloves and a memorial cross I saw as I approached Porthleven.

Foxgloves on the Coast Path between Prussia Cove and Praa Sands.

Foxgloves (*Digitalis purpurea*)

Most people do not think of foxgloves as maritime plants; they are not even mentioned in Ian Hepburn's *Flowers of the Coast* (a Collins New Naturalist book first published in 1952). This very poisonous, hairy plant is better known as an inland plant of hedgerows, heaths and grassy banks. But it is quite common on the cliffs of Cornwall and, surprisingly for such a tall herbaceous plant, remains upright even in the windiest conditions. I have also seen them on Stepper Point, the cliffs near Port Isaac, and several other exposed locations near the Coast Path.

The memorial cross had the following poignant inscription:

This cross has been erected in memory of the many mariners drowned on this part of the coast from time immemorial and buried on the cliff hereabout. Also to commemorate the passing of the 'Gryll's Act' of 1808 since when bodies cast up by the sea have been laid to rest in the nearest consecrated ground. Erected March 1949.

Perhaps I hadn't seen anything else worth stopping for because I was busy keeping to the way-marked path and avoiding the cracks opening up on the cliff tops. Or perhaps I had been spoilt by the spectacular sights of West Penwith. In any case, I arrived at Porthleven at about lunchtime.

Porthleven is a wonderful place to see waves crashing over the clock tower in heavy storms. But today the sea was calm and the streets crowded. I jostled my way quickly through the town, and pressed on to Loe Bar and Loe Pool.

Before the construction of reservoirs, Loe Pool was the largest lake in the south of England. It is a mile and a half (2.4 km) long by half a mile (0.8 km) wide, and renowned for birds and butterflies. Otters also live in and around the lake. It is only separated from the full force of the English Channel by a narrow strip of shingle about 140 metres (150 yards) wide.

This shingle strip is called Loe Bar. Fresh water from the lake percolates through the shingle to the sea. But only rarely, when exceptionally rough storms cause a temporary breach in the beach, does seawater enter the lake .

Shingle is a very harsh environment. It has almost no soil, so plants have difficulty obtaining sufficient nutrients, and fresh water is poorly retained. The salty conditions add to the problems that plants have in obtaining and conserving water. Only specialist plants, such as the yellow horned poppy and the sea holly can survive here.

According to scientists, Loe Bar formed as the result of climate change. The rising sea levels after the last Ice Age (approximately 10,000 years

Loe Bar and the legend of Tregeagle

A more colourful explanation of how Loe Bar and the lake formed is that a terrible ogre called Tregeagle was responsible. There are many stories in Cornwall about Jan Tregeagle. In some he is a giant; in others a man. All agree that he was wicked.

Some claim that Tregeagle was a corrupt steward who lived at Treworder near Wadebridge, and that the legends about him grew because of his cruelty to local tenants. Perhaps the tales of the steward became intermingled with those of a giant.

One legend tells how Tregeagle's dead spirit was summoned, by accident or design, to verify whether a certain loan had been repaid. Having escaped the clutches of the devil, naturally Tregeagle was reluctant to return to them, and refused to leave. To keep him out of mischief, and out of the way of the devil, he was set a series of never-ending tasks.

If the tasks were never-ending, you might ask, why did Tregeagle have to carry out a series of them? The answer is that eventually his loud moans and lamentations at his sad fate would drive the locals to distraction, and he would be asked to move on.

One of his tasks was to move sand from one south-coast cove to another. Poor Tregeagle laboured on, but the sea continually washed away the sand he had put down. Meanwhile, the devil was always on the lookout to recapture him. One day, when Tregeagle was moving his sack full of sand, the devil tripped him and he fell. All the sand spilled from the sack and held back the sea. In this way, Tregeagle created Loe Bar and Loe Pool.

Those of you with a kindly disposition will be pleased to hear that the devil never caught Tregeagle, even after this underhand trick. Some say that he continues his labours to this day.

Sea holly (*Eryngium maritimum*)
This unmistakable perennial plant is well adapted to the harsh, salty, dry conditions of shingle beaches and sand dunes. It can obtain and retain enough water to grow and survive. Its very long (up to 2 metres/8 feet), creeping roots help to tap water supplies; the thick, waxy surfaces of its metallic, bluish-green leaves help it to conserve water. The spines on its leaves also help to reduce water loss, and deter herbivores (and people wishing to sit on the shingle for a picnic). Its main flowering period is July to August.

Henry Trengrouse and the breeches buoy

One of the people who witnessed the wreck of the *Anson* was Henry Trengrouse of Helston. He was so upset by what he saw that he invented a special apparatus. By firing a rocket, a line links a distressed ship to the shore, and a pulley system allows sailors to escape to safety. It took Trengrouse ten years to develop his life-saving invention, before it was officially adopted as standard equipment. Since then the breeches buoy, as the apparatus became known, has saved hundreds of lives.

ago) led to masses of shingle being dumped between two cliffs at the mouth of the River Cober. The flow of the river was effectively blocked allowing a lake to form: this is Loe Pool.

I walked over the shingle beach at Loe Bar, careful not to tread on any sea holly or other precious plants. At the eastern end of the beach, the Coast Path passes a white cross in memory of the loss of a Royal Navy ship.

In 1807, HMS *Anson* ran aground on Loe Bar and broke up. The notorious undertow that occurs off the Bar, making bathing there so dangerous, sucked the sailors out to sea, and about

Church Cove, with the Church of St Winwaloe protected by the headland.

100 officers and men were lost. What made this incident particularly sad was that people on shore saw the disaster unfolding in front of them, but were powerless to prevent it. However, it did inspire the invention of the breeches buoy by a local man, Henry Trengrouse.

Still thinking about Henry Trengrouse and HMS *Anson*, I walked along the Coast Path to Gunwalloe Fishing Cove, and from there up to the top of Halzephron Cliffs, and on to Church Cove. Halzephron means 'Hell's Cliff', and it is an apt name. Many ships have been wrecked on the jagged rocks below. For hundreds of years, drowned sailors were buried unceremoniously in shallow, unmarked graves on the cliff top.

Although drowned bodies are now treated with more respect, the nearby sea is as treacherous and dangerous as ever. However, anyone in distress along this stretch of coast now has the advantage of being close to one of the finest Air-Sea rescue services in the world. The Royal Naval Air Station (RNAS) at Culdrose, near Helston, is the largest helicopter station in Western Europe, and its helicopters rescue many people from the sea and cliffs every year.

*A Culdrose helicopter in action.**

Late in the afternoon, making my way towards Church Cove, I saw a helicopter in action. A man was being winched up from the cliff slopes, probably as part of a training exercise, but possibly because he had got into difficulties. Before I could get close enough to see what was happening, the incident was over, and the helicopter was returning to Culdrose.

From Halzephron Cliff, I continued along the Coast Path and down to the pretty little cove in which the Church of St Winwaloe snuggles.

The Church of St Winwaloe

The church, with its curious detached tower, is in the northern corner of Church Cove. It lies so low to the ground, and so close to the headland, that it appears to be hewn from the rock against which it huddles.

Today, with few houses in sight, it seems an odd place to have such a fine religious building, but things were different in the past. In the Dark Ages, there was a large settlement close by, and the local manor had one of the largest Cornish entries in the Domesday Survey. Although the present church was built in the fourteenth and fifteenth centuries, it was on the same site as a previous church. This probably explains why St Winwaloe's was sited in what is today an isolated spot.

According to local legend, the church was built as a thanksgiving by a survivor of a ship wrecked in Church Cove. Like most legends, this is not without substance: several ships, including a Spanish treasure ship, have come to grief on the rocks nearby.

Then I walked along the beach and crossed a stream in front of the magnificent-looking Mullion Golf Course. Avoiding low-flying golf balls, I took the Coast Path up towards a large, impressive building (now a residential home, but once the Poldhu Hotel), and followed the signs to the Marconi Monument. I stopped to read the inscriptions on the four brass plates. They commemorate the achievements of the Italian Guglielmo Marconi and his team of researchers and engineers at the Poldhu Wireless Station, which was located nearby.

Marconi at Poldhu

Marconi and his associates transmitted the first signals ever conveyed across the Atlantic by wireless telegraphy. They chose Poldhu to carry out their experiment for two main reasons: it provides a clear path for radio waves to cross the Atlantic; and, almost as important, its remote isolation gave some privacy from the prying eyes of reporters and rivals. The signals sent in the first transmission from Poldhu and received at St John's, Newfoundland on 12 December 1901 were a simple repetition of the morse letter 'S'. In 1902, the Marconi team established the first transoceanic wireless telegraphy service across the Atlantic.

The new technology was quickly put to good use. In 1910, Dr Crippin (accused of murdering his wife) was arrested in mid-Atlantic while attempting to escape to Canada, thanks to a wireless message sent from SS *Montrose* to New Scotland Yard via Poldhu. Two years later, wireless was the means by which calls for help were sent from the stricken liner *Titanic*.

Mullion Cove and its nineteenth-century harbour.

By the time I had read the inscriptions and had a look (from the outside) at the Marconi Wireless Station, it was getting dark and time to head for Mullion Cove.

I had hoped to find bed and breakfast accommodation at the Cove, but when I arrived there was none available. So, feeling rejected, I trudged up to Predannack with no more than a cursory look around the Cove. However, I returned in November when I had more time to see the tiny harbour with its picturesque net store.

As I made the giddy climb out of Mullion Cove, I noticed that the vegetation changed with the underlying geology. Up to Mullion Cove, I had been walking on schist – flaky metamorphic rocks – now I was entering a landscape dominated by serpentine.

I passed Mullion Island – the most important site on the Lizard for many seabirds, including cormorants, shags, razorbills, guillemots, black-backed gulls and kittiwakes. Unfortunately it was becoming too dark to get a good view of them.

Towards the top of Mullion Cliff, I took the footpath that goes inland through a nature reserve past Predannack Manor Farm. From there, after a few unintentional detours, I found Teneriffe Farm, my destination. I put up my tent in record time, had a simple meal, and retired for the night.

The harbour at Mullion Cove

Mullion Cove is dominated by its harbour. It was built between 1893 and 1895 with money from Lord Robartes of Lanhydrock, who wanted to compensate the Mullion fishermen after several bad pilchard harvests. The harbour is now managed by the National Trust, which also owns the winch house and the quaint net store.

The harbour faces west, straight into the prevailing winds. Consequently, the walls are regularly damaged during ferocious winter gales. The costs of repairs are met by various funds administered by the National Trust, but as stated in one of the Trust's leaflets (Coast of Cornwall, No.13, *The Lizard, West Coast*) this is '...a cost which some might argue is increasingly difficult to justify.'

Day 11 (18.4 ml/30.5 km)

Mullion to Godrevy Cove

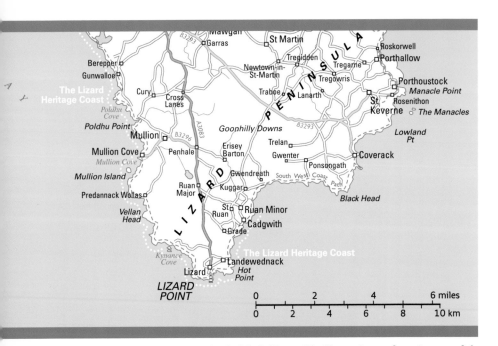

Breakfast eaten, tent packed, I left Teneriffe Farm just after 6 a.m., followed the track down to Windyridge Farm, and from there made my way to the Coast Path that leads to Kynance Cove. Despite the drizzle, I was excited about the prospect of walking along what many regard as the most spectacular part of the Cornish coast.

I had gone only a short distance before I entered the land belonging to Kynance Farm. Its maritime heath and grassland supports a long list of rare and unusual plants, including spring sandwort, a variety of orchids, harebells, and more than a dozen species of clover. One Victorian naturalist claimed that he found 12 different species lying under a hat that he had dropped on the ground. Most of the plants are low-lying, so that they can hug the ground and avoid the worst effects of the winds that sweep over the flat and open Lizard plateau.

Kynance Cove, on the Lizard peninsula.

As wild and natural as the landscape appears, it would soon turn into rough scrub and woodland if it were not for human interference. Indeed, the Lizard heath is manmade: it originated from woodland cleared by our Bronze Age ancestors, who then used it mainly for grazing.

In the twentieth century, modern farming techniques threatened a serious decline in the heathland. I saw this first-hand in the 1970s when I was employed for a short time by the Nature Conservancy Council to carry out a survey of the heath on the Lizard. One of my tasks was to identify the areas in which its three species of heather grew: Cornish heath, bell heather, and cross-leaved heath.

Although all three heathers were still growing in profusion, the area of heathland was declining rapidly in the 1970s because of changes in farming practice – in particular, the use of heavy diggers to remove hedgerows, and to push large gabbro blocks to field margins. Gabbro is similar to granite. It forms large blocks which, when in the middle of fields, make ploughing very difficult. Pushing them to field margins converted land from grazing to arable.

In the 1980s, the decline in heathland was reversed when the area became a part of the Kynance National Nature Reserve. Kynance acquired its status of National Nature Reserve because of the mix of habitats (cliffs, maritime heathland and coastal grassland) that make it unique in Britain. Today, the land around Kynance Farm is managed sensitively to encourage wildlife. Winter scrub clearance, periodic controlled burning, and grazing by highland cattle are some of the techniques used.

Highland cattle

This ancient breed of shaggy-pelted Scottish cattle is also known as long-horn and hielon coo, but its most descriptive name is *hairy coo*.

The breed is an ideal choice for helping to conserve the Lizard heath. It's very hardy, able to live outside in all seasons, and has a long breeding life. But its unfussy eating habits are probably its most important asset. Highland cattle will eat plants that other cattle avoid. In their search for food, they use their long horns to push scrub out of the way, and trample over bracken and brambles. In addition to grazing on grasses, they browse the succulent shoots of invasive weeds which would otherwise need to be controlled by more costly, or less environmentally friendly, means.

Not only do they benefit nature conservation, these wonderfully shaggy beasts are a delight to see in such a spectacular setting.

Bloody cranesbill
(*Geranium sanguineum*)

At Kynance, the bloody cranesbill forms compact hummocks. Usually, this plant grows on mineral-rich, alkaline grass-lands. It is more commonly associated with limestone platforms than with the Cornish cliffs, but the special geology of the Lizard provides the minerals on which the bloody cranesbill thrives.

Walking along parts of the cliff-top Coast Path to Kynance was as easy as treading barefoot on a carpet, it was so soft and low cut. Some of the paths around Kynance are specially mown, not for the comfort of cliff walkers, but to act as firebreaks.

Of the many flowering plants around Kynance, the one that attracted my attention most was the bloody cranesbill (*Geranium sanguineum*). This is not the rarest plant, but from June to about August, its magenta-purple flowers make it one of the most brilliant.

When I arrived at Kynance Cove, the persistent drizzle and a rising tide hid much of the foreshore. I was unable to explore the area around the islets, the largest of which is Asparagus Island.

The rocks and pebbles of Kynance Cove are composed of serpentine, both red and green-mottled, and granite. Wetting a pebble reveals the beauty of the varied colours.

From Kynance, I went up the cliff path, skirted Pentreath Beach, and arrived at Lizard Point, the most southerly tip of Britain, before 10 a.m.

Asparagus Island

The Island is named after the plant that grows there. This is not the cultivated variety eaten with butter on toast, but the bitter-tasting, barely edible wild asparagus (*Asparagus prostratus*).

Wild asparagus is a perennial plant with underground rhizomes of tubers. As its shoots die back in winter, it's easiest to spot in late spring when it produces a bushy growth, and in autumn when it has glossy red berries.

Over-trampling, lack of grazing, and farming with fertilizers have contributed to the decline of wild asparagus. According to Ian Bennalick, a botanist with the CWT, there were a dozen or so colonies on Asparagus Island when it was last surveyed.

Wild asparagus is rare. It is found in only 28 sites across the UK, on coastal dunes as well as sea cliffs, usually within 100 metres (110 yards) of the open sea. Only one site occurs outside South Wales and Cornwall. This is in Dorset, and consists of only one female plant. It can reproduce vegetatively using its rhizomes, but this has the serious disadvantage of limiting its variation. In 2006, a botanist was employed to give the Dorset plant a helping hand by using the mature pollen of male asparagus plants from Asparagus Island to pollinate the Dorset plant, 200 km (125 miles) away.

Even the colonies on Asparagus Island are under threat. Not from trampling or fertilizers, but from the Hottentot fig, *Caprobrotus edulis* (left) – an attractive but invasive plant introduced to British gardens in 1690 from South West Africa. It is such a serious threat to native wild plants that National Trust wardens have resorted to abseiling down cliffs to remove it.

By avoiding the paths leading into Lizard Town, I had missed the opportunity to go to The Lizard Pasty Shop. However, this omission was rectified when I returned to have a more relaxed look around the Lizard in November, and to try one of Ann Muller's famous and delicious pasties.

Back in June, drizzle had turned to rain, so after a quick look around Polpeor Cove, I sought shelter and sustenance in The Most Southerly Café.

Polpeor Cove and the Lizard lifeboat

Looking down on Polpeor Cove you see what appears to be a lifeboat house. The Lizard lifeboat was kept in three different places, and this was the last one. It incorporated a turntable so the lifeboat could be housed with its bow facing the sea, ready for a speedy launching. The other two places are at a higher level. One is now the winch house, the other was at the top of the cliff.

Each change of site brought improvements in efficiency, but the very exposed position of Polpeor Cove always made launching a very risky business. In 1961 the lifeboat station was transferred to Kilcobben, near Church Cove. Although a more sheltered site and safer for launching, the cliff at Kilcobben is so steep that a lift had to be constructed to carry the crew to and from the lifeboat house.

Today, the Polpeor complex is owned by the Polpeor Boathouse Committee, and the slipway is used by local fishermen to moor their boats.

Close to the café was a sign from the Cornish Chough Project (a partnership of the RSPB, the National Trust and Natural England). I read the news about the four young fledges and their parents, and was tempted by the invitation to 'See Cornwall's most charismatic bird at Southerly point...' where 'Information Wardens are on hand to show you the birds through high quality optics as they fly to and from their nesting cave.' But wanting to reach Coverack by late afternoon, I couldn't take up the offer.

However, I did go to the workshop of P.L. Casley & Son, serpentine specialists, before stepping out to the lighthouse behind Polbream Cove.

Serpentine

The Lizard is unusual in having a combination of mild climate and a large expanse of flat land close to the sea, but what makes it unique is its geology. Although geologists generally agree about the composition of its rocks, there is much dispute about how the different rock types came to the Lizard, and what caused them to become so intimately intermingled. Most explanations involve a cataclysmic collision between great land masses, and the subsequent release of enormous quantities of igneous material formed under very high pressures and temperatures within the bowels of the Earth.

Serpentine is probably the most famous rock type formed at the Lizard under these violent conditions. It is generally a dark green or red rock (above, with barnacles), with attractive veining, and acquired its name from having a texture similar to snakeskin. Serpentine is thought to have originated in the Earth's mantle deep under an ocean that vanished when the land masses collided. When the igneous material was extruded into the ancient ocean, it was subjected to a low-temperature process. This involved its original minerals combining with water to form new minerals.

As well as producing thin, magnesium-rich soils which support a wonderful maritime heathland, serpentine is extraordinarily attractive. Being relatively soft, it is easily carved or turned on a lathe to make ornaments. P.L. Casley & Son, and other local craftsmen, are continuing a long tradition. Lizard craftsmen have been working serpentine commercially since at least the 1820s. After a visit to Penzance in 1846, Queen Victoria acquired several items for Osborne House. The Queen was *the* major trend-setter of her day; where she went, others followed, and what she acquired, others wanted to have, so serpentine sales received a significant boost. The item that caught my eye was a magnificent miniature lighthouse, about three feet high. It took about two weeks to make.

Serpentine is not only used to make ornaments. It has been extracted from quarries north of Church Cove to make firebrick, and to provide stones to build runways at RNAS Culdrose. It has also been used to make stiles and other useful objects.

The Lizard lighthouse.

The Lizard lighthouse

The earliest beacon to guide mariners through the harzardous seas off Lizard Point was completed by Sir John Killigrew, a philanthropist from Falmouth, in the Christmas of 1619. He sponsored it himself, hoping to be recompensed by voluntary contributions from passing mariners. But he received insufficient funds to maintain the lighthouse. James I intervened by imposing a mandatory fee on all vessels passing the light. This provoked such opposition from ship owners that the light was extinguished and the tower demolished.

It was not until 1751 that another lighthouse was erected. It consisted of two distinctive towers, between which was a cottage. Apparently, the cottage housed an overlooker who would lie on a couch positioned so that he could see both lights. If for any reason the coal-fired lights dimmed, he would blast a cow-horn as a signal for the bellow-blowers to increase their efforts.

Trinity House has been responsible for the lighthouse since 1771. Structural alterations made in 1812 left the station looking much as it does today. In the same year, oil lamps replaced the coal-fired lamps. These were themselves replaced in 1878, when a steam-driven generator supplied energy to ignite two electric arc lamps. In 1924, an electrified beam from a light 70 metres (230 feet) above mean high water was installed. The light shines so brilliantly that it has a range of 26 nautical miles (48 km).

The light was automated in 1998, but you can visit the lighthouse – except on Sundays and on foggy days, when the giant foghorns are blasting out their warning.

After passing in front of the lighthouse, I encountered what Wilkie Collins, in *Rambles Beyond Railways* (1851), described as '... a hideous chasm in the cliff, sunk to a perpendicular depth of seventy feet, and measuring more than 100 feet in circumference.' The National Trust has left the area known as the Lion's Den unfenced, so that the spectacle can be enjoyed without the intrusion of a barrier, but there are many signs warning visitors not to get too close to the edge.

This dangerous but spectacular hole formed in 1847 from the sudden overnight collapse of a sea cave. Although hundreds of tons of soil and rock must have fallen, the whole event apparently happened so quietly that nobody noticed until the following morning.

This incident demonstrates how quickly the details of our coastal scenery can change. It is still a 'work in progress', and special care should be taken when walking close to the edge of eroding cliffs, for we cannot be sure when the next dramatic landslip might occur.

The lookout station at Bass Point.

Having survived my visit to the Lion's Den, I moved on to Bass Point where there is a lookout station. This belonged to HM Coastguard until the Government closed it down. In 1994 a group of local people, concerned that two local fishermen drowned within sight of the unmanned coastguard station, reopened it on a voluntary basis. It became the Bass Point Station of the National Coastwatch Institute, and is run by volunteers who keep an eye on the local waters and cliffs, and inform HM Coastguard at Falmouth if anyone is in difficulties. Its other roles include providing daily weather reports to the Coastguard and BBC Radio Cornwall; advising Lloyds of London of Commercial shipping traffic, and liaising with conservation agencies about movements of wildlife and pollution incidents.

On my way to Kilcobben Cove, I passed what was the Lloyd's Signalling Station. Until the advent of radio communication, all sea traffic going up the English Channel had to come close to the Lizard in order to signal their passage. One captain who resented having to make this dangerous manoeuvre is reported as saying, 'If they would sink Lloyd's signalling station, there would be no more wrecks on the Manacles or around Lizard Head, because captains would then give that corner a wide berth.' The Lloyds Signalling Station was not sunk, but when it was closed the station was sold and became a private residence. Ships no longer have to come so close to the Lizard Point to signal their passage. The incidence of wrecks has declined, but not as much as the captain had hoped.

At Kilcobben Cove I had a quick look down at the new Lifeboat station that has replaced both the Lizard and Cadgwith stations. Although I saw the lift in action, I was disappointed not to see its most recent all-weather lifeboat, the 47-foot (14.3-metre), twin-engined *David Robinson*.

Veering left after leaving the lifeboat station, I stopped to look at a bronze plaque on a single bench. I had read many on my journey so far. Most had dedications in memory of people, some famous, who had really loved a particular stretch of coast. Many of them contained

New Lifeboat station, Kilcobben Cove.*

messages that tugged at the heart strings, and made you realize how much joy the Cornish coast has given people. But the dedication on this bench was the most curious. It said simply: HSM UNSWORTH (POPEYE),1920–1998 MISBEHAVED ALL HIS LIFE.

I left the bench intrigued by what might 'Popeye' might have done to deserve such an epitaph. On my return home, my attempts to discover more about this man have been unsuccessful – even Wikipedia offers no information. I therefore remain as intrigued as I was when I made my way downhill to Church Cove.

Church Cove has several interesting features, but my mind was still boggled by Popeye's epitaph. I started thinking of characters (including one or two of my close relations) who might deserve the same memorial. I took little notice of the Capstan House, the pilchard palace at Church Cove, nor anything else until I reached a National Trust sign that marked my arrival at the Devil's Frying Pan.

Like the Lion's Den, this funnel-shaped depression was probably formed from a cave collapsing along fault lines. However, the more advanced state of erosion of the Devil's Frying Pan makes it easier to see and to photograph.

The Devil's Frying Pan.*

Cadgwith – a beautiful village nestling in a sheltered bay.

Leaving the Frying Pan, I continued down to Cadgwith, a beautiful village nestling in a sheltered bay.

Although the most prominent buildings in Cadgwith are delightful thatched holiday cottages, it is still an active fishing cove with a fleet of eight medium-sized vessels. Five vessels are involved in potting for crabs and lobsters and netting for fish; two operate as netters only, and the other one is a potter. The netting includes some seining for pilchards. However, pilchard catches are tiny compared with the record daily catch of 1,300,000 pilchards made during the nineteenth century when the pilchard fishery was at its peak.

The waters around Cadgwith attract one of the largest fish of all – the basking shark. It was once a target for fishermen, prized for its rich stores of liver oil, but it is now a fully protected species in UK waters.

I had heard reports of sightings of basking sharks off the East Lizard when I left Cape Cornwall. I had seen the characteristic dorsal fins of a pair off Gwennap Head as I made my way to Porthcurno, but it was just off Cadgwith that Gavin Parsons managed to take his stunning close-up underwater photograph of a gentle giant feeding.

From Cadgwith, I walked to Carleon Cove, below the pretty hamlet of Poltesco. At the Cove, I looked at the ruins of the old serpentine works and the round building which once housed the capstan that hauled boats and their nets out of the water.

I proceeded as quickly as I could towards Coverack, on my way passing along Kennack Sands where there is another raised beach (see also

The basking shark
(*Cetorhinus maximus*)

Gavin Parsons, a wildlife photographer and keen diver, took his photograph of a basking shark while snorkelling off Cadgwith, near the old lifeboat house. He was careful not to alarm the shark, hence his use of a snorkel rather than underwater breathing apparatus as this releases gas bubbles that might disturb the fish. This wonderful animal had come close to the shore to filter-feed on zooplankton – small marine animals that drift from one place to another in the water currents.

Basking sharks can grow more than 10 metres (33 feet) in length, and may weigh up to 7 tonnes (6.8 tons). They are the largest wild animal found regularly in Britain. They process up to 6,000 litres (1,320 gallons) of plankton-rich seawater per hour through their mouths, and use modified gill-rakers to filter out the animals. They are commonly sighted around Cornwall during the summer, sometimes in schools of 100 or more; it is staggering to think how rich the zooplankton must be to support such large numbers. Basking sharks are rarely seen in Cornish waters during the winter. It is not clear where they go.

Porth Nanven, page 89). Much of the rest my walk along Treleaver Cliff, Black Head and Chynallis Cliff was on land owned by the National Trust, which uses hardy Shetland ponies to graze the cliff slopes and control the scrub.

I arrived at Coverack's small harbour in the early evening. With a few daylight hours still remaining I decided to try to get to Porthoustock or Porthallow before nightfall.

I followed the road along the seafront and headed for Lowland Point, yet another raised beach, and continued along the Coast Path as far as Dean Quarries. As blasting had stopped for the day, and no red flags were flying, I was able to follow the way-marked route through the quarry to reach Dean Point, south of Godrevy Cove.

The walk from Coverack to Godrevy Cove had taken me longer than expected. Too tired to go much further, I decided to pitch my tent at the

A Shetland pony on Treleaver Cliff

A Shetland pony – one of a herd introduced by the National Trust on to the cliffs between Cadgwith and Coverack to promote the growth of rare and interesting flowering plants. These plants include autumn squill, long-headed clover, and Cornish heath. The cross in the photograph commemorates a young crew member killed in a helicopter crash in 1974.

The harbour at Coverack.*

The sand hopper (*Talitrus saltator*)
Sand hoppers are crustaceans – the same group to which woodlice, prawns, crabs and lobsters belong. They are sometimes called sand fleas because of the way they jump around. Unless disturbed by trampling feet, they usually spend the day in burrows up to 30 cm (1 ft) deep, in the sand above high-water mark.

When I walked down the sandy shore at about 10 p.m., most had emerged from their burrows and were moving in their many thousands down the beach to feed on debris and decaying seaweed. When the tide comes in, the sand hoppers make their way back up the shore.

top of the beach on a flat patch of dune well above high water. Godrevy seemed secluded. There were no people about. I anticipated an uninterrupted night's sleep.

Before settling down in my sleeping bag, I cooked a meal of rice and pilchards, and while waiting for the water to boil, went down towards the water's edge to see what marine life was active on the sandy shore.

During the day, a sandy shore can appear lifeless as most animals hide from the heat of the sun or from predators. But as soon as dusk falls they come out of hiding to find food and carry out other essential activities. I found one such animal in great abundance: the sand hopper (*Talitrus saltator*).

While I was eating, someone made a determined bee-line for the tent. It turned out to be the farmer who owned the land above the

*Dean Quarry.**

beach which, he informed me, was private. Having entered the beach via the Dean Quarry, I had not seen the notices on the Coast Path from Rose-nithon. I was quite willing to decamp, but he very considerately allowed me to stay the night. We chatted for a while. He told me that he used to allow overnight campers, but some people brought whole families down to the beach to camp in large tents for long weekends, and some of their habits were far from sanitary – hence his ban. We parted on friendly terms, and I looked forward to that uninterrupted sleep.

When I pitched my tent, I noticed the forbidding cluster of rocks off-shore. My map told me that they were the Manacles – the most notorious rocks on the south coast. I remembered that St Keverne church has more than 400 of the Manacles' shipwreck victims in its graveyard. What I did not remember was that in calm weather the rocks are a popular area for fishing from boats. And I did not know that Godrevy Cove is equally popu-lar among shore anglers. It was a calm night; the tide was coming in, and it was starting to rain – ideal conditions for a bit of night fishing.

Just after midnight, my deep sleep was suddenly interrupted by the sound of wellingtons making their way down the beach, and cries of 'I've got one!', and 'Damn, it's got away!', from boats offshore. Peering out of the tent, I was confronted by what looked like a swarm of fireflies. Lights were whizzing past my vision, presumably attached to lines or men that I could not see. As the rain was getting heavier, I thought fishing would be aborted, but the anglers and fishermen carried on undeterred until at least 1.30 a.m. when, at last, I fell asleep again. (For anyone more interested in what they were catching than in my lack of sleep, it was sea bass.)

Day 12 (22 ml/35.4 km)

Godrevy Cove to Falmouth

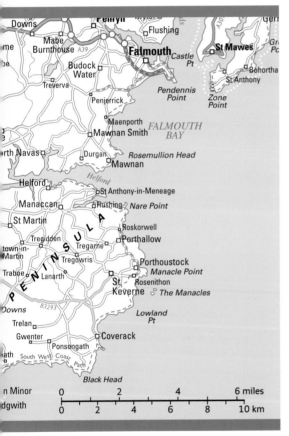

It was pouring with rain for most of the night, but it had stopped when I got up at about 5.30 a.m. Taking advantage of the lull in the storm, I decided to get everything packed and depart before the rain returned. Just as I was putting the last few items in my rucksack, the heavens opened again. It was a wet walk up the sunken path and gravel track towards Rosenithon, becoming even wetter as I crossed the fields and went down the road to Porthoustock. I was intrigued by the curious structures on the north and south sides of its cove, and returned in the autumn to find out more about them.

I took the official South West Coast Path route to Porthallow. It was inland and involved some road walking, but seemed easier to follow than the alternative coastal route via Porthkerris beach.

At Porthallow I found out that its beach was purchased from the Trelowarren Estate by the village community, who now manage it. They obtain funds from visitors parking their cars at the top of the beach, and by holding various fund-raising events including a fishing fête in the summer. Curious to find out how good the management was, I looked around beach. It shelved deeply, and was covered with grey stones and pebbles (presumably thrown back by the sea from the quarries further south). I didn't find it particularly inviting, but it did look well cared for.

Porthoustock developed as a port for the nearby stone quarries in the 1890s.

Before leaving Porthallow, I would have liked to see 'the interesting pictures of Manacles wrecks' that one of the guidebooks said were displayed in the Five Pilchards Inn, but as it wasn't open I returned to the official Coast Path and headed north-west to the large mass of Nare Head and Nare Point beyond.

To my relief, the path once again followed the cliff closely, making it easy to follow. As I passed above Nare Cove, I noticed a distinct change in the surrounding geology. Slates and granite had replaced the serpentine, gneiss and schist that characterize the Lizard.

Apparently there are fine views from Nare Head, but low cloud prevented me from seeing much. I rounded Nare Point and turned west to Gillan Creek.

Many small boats were moored in the mouth of Gillan Creek, taking advantage of its sheltered position.

Porthoustock

Porthoustock originated as a fishing hamlet. Several small craft still operate from its shingle beach, mainly long-lining but with some potting for crabs and lobsters and some net fishing. The main function of Porthoustock changed in the 1890s when it developed as a port for the nearby stone quarries. Today, vessels up to 82 metres (270 feet) long can come alongside the wharf on the southern side of the beach to be loaded with stone from the adjacent quarries. The stone is mainly diorite – a dark green, igneous rock like granite, but without quartz. The curious large concrete structure on the northern side of the beach is a disused stone mill that used to process large, locally extracted stones.

Boats moored in the mouth of Gillan Creek. *

Gillan Creek. *

There was once a medieval port on the north side of the creek, but the harbour is now silted up. Although there's no ferry, the creek can be crossed on foot one hour either side of low tide. When I arrived, the tide was ebbing, but the water was still too high for me to wade. Rather than take the road route to Helford via Manaccan, I scrambled along the shore to Flushing to look for the crossing place and wait.

Flushing was a bit of a disappointment. Its group of houses set in oak and pine woods is pleasant enough, but much less grand than I had expected. I had vague memories from childhood that Flushing was an elegant village of Queen Anne houses. When I studied my map, I realized that these memories must be of the other, larger Flushing opposite Falmouth.

When the water had ebbed sufficiently, I found the crossing place opposite St Anthony-in-Meneage church, removed my boots, and paddled across.

Once across Gillan Creek, I meandered my way through gates and fields to Dennis Head, the site of a prehistoric earthworks as well as a fortification with gun emplacements. In 1646, the Royalist force which manned the fortification surrendered, leaving Cromwell's Roundheads to march on Falmouth.

*St Anthony-in-Meneage from Gillan Creek.**

The Church of St Anthony-in-Meneage

The Church of St Anthony-in-Meneage is built on what was probably an early Christian site. The Cornish word *meneage* means 'land of monks', and the site was mentioned in tenth-century documents.

According to Claude Berry in his book *Cornwall* (1949), the church was built '... to the glory of the saint by the owner of a ship overtaken by a storm in the Channel. Praying for succour to St Anthony, he promised to give a church if his petition was granted; and the saint then saw to it that the vessel survived wind and sea and came safely to berth in Gillan Harbour.'

The emblem of St Anthony is a pig and, according to one guidebook, locals are sometimes called 'St Anthony Pigs'.

From Dennis Head, I walked to Helford, passing through the thick woods that line the south bank of the river.

Before going down into the village to find the ferry, I climbed the hill for a good view of the Helford River. I would have liked to explore some of its inlets. Frenchman's Creek gave its name to one of Daphne du Maurier's novels, and Porthnavas Creek is where Helford's famous oyster beds are sited; but to visit them would have taken too long. In any case, it was not as if I had never seen these places before. About 30 years ago, when I was carrying out research into an oyster disease, I had spent some time on the Helford, and even had the privilege of going out with the oyster fishermen to dredge for the delectable bivalves.

The Helford River.

A little egret.

Thinking of delicious oysters, I went down into Helford. On the way I spotted a little egret in a creek. These birds used to be rare spring migrants from mainland Europe, but in recent years they have become permanent residents, and are now quite common in Cornish estuaries. In 2006 about a dozen pairs were breeding in the Helford. I regularly see little egrets feeding in streams and pools on the Camel, but familiarity has not dimmed their enchantment.

At Helford, I went past The Shipwright's Arms, and along the private path to the ferry point. To summon the ferry, I had to make sure that a red circle was not displayed at Helford Passage, then I swang open the semicircular black board at the ferry point to make a yellow circle. With this signal, the ferry returned to Helford and took me across to the sand and shingle beach at Helford Passage.

From here, I went eastwards along the beach, climbed some steps, and then rejoined the Coast Path which goes below the National Trust's Glendurgan Garden. The Garden has a maze but, as I've proven several times on this trip, I need no such help getting lost, so I continued to Rosemullion Head. Although there's a short cut across its neck, I fancied looking at the views and took the path around the headland.

Helford oyster (*Ostrea edulis*)

Helford oysters belong to the molluscan species *Ostrea edulis*, commonly called native oysters. They are filter-feeding bivalves (their shell is divided into two hinged parts) that live on the sea bed in the estuary, and have been collected as food for centuries. Today, they are dredged from deeper water in the estuary from 1 November to 31 March, and re-laid to fatten on inshore beds in the creeks. The fattening helps oysters become plump and succulent.

An oyster has a very peculiar sex life. Usually it starts as a male, changes to a female as it grows, and may change sex several times during its life. Some individuals can be male and female at the same time.

Natives breed in the summer, during which time they divert most of their resources to reproducing (hence the ban against collecting them when there is no 'r' in the month).

The larvae that result from the breeding spend about two weeks drifting as plankton in the sea, then they develop their shells and settle as spat. From that time on, they never move again unless disturbed by tides, waves, or oyster dredgermen.

In the nineteenth century native oysters were very cheap, and marketed as a poor person's food. Today they are relatively expensive. Farmed Japanese oysters (*Crassostrea gigas*) are a cheaper alternative, but most gourmets do not regard them as such a great delicacy as the natives.

One gourmet described fresh oysters as 'infused with the taste of the sea'; another said that an oyster dish was like '... a beach on a plate'. The 'proper' way to eat oysters is raw, cooled with ice and served with a squeeze of lemon. If you want to add to the exclusiveness of the dish, accompany it with a decent champagne. However, many people prefer to eat them cooked.

When I collected oysters for my research, there always seemed to be a few left over. These invariably ended up as the main ingredient in a simple dish called 'angels on horseback'. The oysters were wrapped in bacon with a cocktail stick to hold the bacon and oyster together, and then toasted under a grill. Served simply on toast, they were absolutely delicious.

I was about halfway around when I saw a herd of bullocks blocking my way some 50 metres ahead. I turned round to take a nearby alternative path when I heard a sound that brought back memories of cowboy films – the thunder of cattle hooves. I looked back and saw the bullocks bearing down on me in a charge (I'm tempted to call it a stampede, but I wouldn't want to be accused of exaggerating). I'm not sure what caused this errant behaviour. Perhaps it was a sudden movement I had made, or perhaps with a rucksack on my back and walking stick in my hand I appeared like some strange beast (Merryn has made this observation several times). Whatever it was, they were spooked. I had no six-shooter to turn them away. All I had was a vague memory that if I were to face them, and stand resolute with arms waving, the frisky bullocks would take one look at me and stop in their tracks. But I was not prepared to test this

Helford Passage.

theory, and I made an undignified escape into the nearest gorse thicket. When the bullocks had moved off to graze elsewhere, and the dust had settled, I counted my limbs (all present and as correct as they ever will be); examined my wounds (a few scratches, which would grow into deep scars by the time I told the story in the pub), and continued towards Falmouth.

My route took me to the stony little cove of Maen Porth, then along the bottom of a golf course to Pennance Point, and on to the wide, sandy beach at Swanpool. Not fancying a boating trip on the reed-rimmed pond, nor a rest in a multi-coloured deckchair, I went on to Gyllyngvase beach.

The last time I had been to Gyllyngvase beach was for a seaweed workshop, during which we had collected various specimens from the rocks and pools. When massed together in collecting buckets, they were just ugly, slimy heaps. When separated out in white enamel dishes of clear seawater, they were transformed into things of great beauty.

I hurried from Gyllyngvase beach, and cut across the town to the Prince of Wales Pier on Albert Quay, arriving just ten minutes after the last ferry had left for St Mawes. This was yet another fine example of my meticulous planning.

I had had in mind to meet my sister Yvonne at St Mawes, and spend the night at her home near the King Harry Ferry. As this was not possible, I was stranded in Falmouth for the night.

Falmouth is a town that has more than most – one of the most historic harbours in the world; decent shops; varied restaurants; good beaches, and even its own castle; but I had little chance to sample these. My priority before nightfall was to obtain bed and breakfast accommodation.

Seaweeds: under water their fronds spread out to display their full beauty.

In the town, most places had displayed their 'No Vacancies' sign even before they saw me coming. Those with vacancies only had double rooms available. I was quite happy to use these, but the proprietors wanted the full double room rate, even though it was unlikely they would get anyone else seeking accommodation at such a late hour. Concluding that the proprietors must have rejected the wisdom embodied in the proverb 'A bird in the hand...' , I went back towards Gyllyngvase beach. On my way I struck gold – a very fine guesthouse called Gayhurst, run by a lady who originates from Port Isaac, and one that actually welcomes walkers.

Seaweeds
Although seaweeds photosynthesize their own food and produce bubbles of oxygen, they are not technically plants. They lack roots, stems and leaves, and have no specialized tissue for transporting water or food. In a biologist's classification of life, they belong to a separate kingdom – the algae – which come in a multitude of colours, shapes and sizes. Those on the rocks of Gyllyngvase beach belong to three main groups: the red, brown and green algae. Some algae are microscopic, yet are vitally important items in the marine ecosystem. They are at the base of all of the food chains of sea fish. Ultimately, even a basking shark depends on these organisms, which are millions of times smaller than itself.

Too late and too tired to go back into town for a restaurant meal, I went to the nearest shop, bought some bread, cheese, olives and wine, filled my belly and went to bed.

Day 13 (13.7 ml/22 km)

Falmouth to Portloe

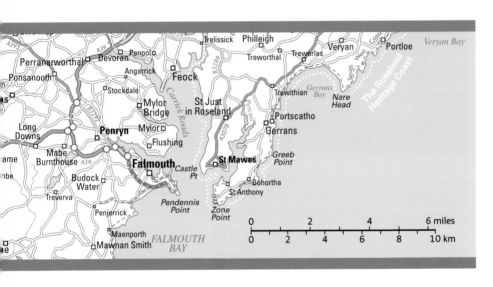

After a superb full English breakfast, I left the guesthouse and retraced my steps to Albert Quay. I needed to hurry to catch the first ferry of the day to St Mawes, and so had no time to see the sights of Falmouth town.

Arriving on the ferry just before its advertised 10 a.m. departure time, we had to wait while a shipment of several cases of locally pressed apple juice was loaded. The ferry left ten minutes late... if only it had done that the previous evening... .

Pushing such futile speculations to the back of my mind, I took advantage of the ferry ride to have a seal's eye view of the waterfront of Falmouth harbour and the entry into St Mawes. With the weather fine and the sea calm, conditions were ideal, and there was little risk of seasickness. This came as a great relief to someone who has to take pills before crossing the Tamar Bridge.

The first I saw of St Mawes was the Castle commanding the harbour entrance. The Castle was referred to in Pope's guide as 'Henry VIII's most decorative Fort'. It was built in 1538, with Pendennis Castle on the other side of the estuary, to protect Falmouth from French invasion. Both castles

*Falmouth harbour, the third largest natural harbour in the world.**

Falmouth harbour

Falmouth was originally two small fishing villages: Pennycomequick and Smithick. Its transformation into a port of global significance really started in 1688, when it became the headquarters for the Post Office Packet Service. By 1808 there were up to 39 Post Office boats sailing regularly from Falmouth to the north of Spain, the Mediterranean, and both North and South America.

Falmouth is said to be the third largest natural harbour in the world. Despite this, its importance as a port gradually declined in the twentieth century. Occasionally, large vessels still call at the port, and the repair yards can be busy, but the exceptionally large waterfront with its deep docking facilities appeared to be much underused when I surveyed them. Perhaps the Government's drive for power to be harnessed from off-shore waves will result in ships equipped with turbines having to go from the port into the Celtic Sea, and Falmouth's fortunes will flourish once again.

came under seige in the Civil War. The Roundhead commander Fairfax took St Mawes for Parliament in 1641, but Pendennis resisted seige for five months – the last Royalist stronghold in Cornwall, and the last but one in England.

St Mawes Castle, at the entrance to Carrick Roads.

After disembarking in St Mawes harbour, it took only a few steps to transfer on to the little ferry that runs to Place House (page 140). This short boat journey meant I could avoid the nine-mile (14.5 km) walking route around the Percuil River. As much of the route is on roads, I was not sorry.

It was on the seaweed-covered shores near Place that I saw my first otter in the wild. This was in the late 1970s, at a time when there was only a remnant population in Cornwall, and they were becoming extinct in most other counties. The decline coincided with an increase in the

number of mink escaping from farms. Therefore it was easy to conclude that the mink were causing the decline.

Meticulous veterinary research showed that this conclusion was wrong; much of the decline was due to pesticides, such as organochlorines and polychlorinated biphenyls. These found their way into rivers and streams, accumulated in the food chain, and were taken up by the otters, causing their endocrine glands to malfunction.

One of the leading researchers into the causes of otter mortalities is veterinary pathologist Vic Simpson, who has been carrying out post-mortems on otters from Cornwall and elsewhere since the 1980s. In 2001, in partnership with the CWT, he established Britain's first ever Wildlife Veterinary Investigation Centre, which is based in Cornwall.

Otters thrive in the Fal.

The otter research contributed to a ban on the use of certain pesticides. Since the ban, the otter has made a slow but successful recovery. Populations in and around the Fal are now thriving, despite a new threat discovered in 2005. A flatworm parasite, thought to have been introduced in ornamental fish from Eastern Europe and Russia, was spreading throughout the otter population in southern England. The spread coincided with a dramatic increase in otter deaths on the Somerset Plains.

Vic and other otter researchers are trying to find out if these deaths are related to the parasite, or to something else altogether. The results of their work will help us to maintain a healthy population in Cornwall.

The seaweeds on rocky shores around Place House are dominated by brown wracks. In the past, before the widespread use of artificial fertilizers, these weeds would have been gathered from the shore and used to add nutrients to nearby fields.

Bladder wrack (*Fucus vesiculosus*) and knotted wrack (*Ascophylum nodousm*)
The two main brown weeds at Place are the bladderwrack (*Fucus vesiculosus*), and the egg or knotted wrack (*Ascophylum nodousm*). Each has air bladders. In the bladderwrack they are arranged in pairs either side of the midrib, down its frond (the leaf-like structure). The air bladders of the knotted wrack are arranged singly down the frond. In both, the air bladders support the fronds in the water to give them maximum exposure to sunlight for photosynthesis. This function is more important in sheltered waters than in exposed situations, where waves keep the fronds afloat. Consequently, the air bladders change in size and number according to the exposure. On the more exposed shores towards St Anthony Head, they tend to be smaller and fewer than in the very sheltered creeks such as at Place.

I have been to the Percuil River many times to search for marine animals. At one particular location, the sea has intruded into the shelter of the estuary and brought with it all manner of wonderful creatures usually found only in much deeper water. There you will find peculiar polychaete worms, including sea mice and fan worms, burrowing sea anemones and vase-shaped tunicates (better known as sea squirts, for their habit of jet-propelling water at intruders when disturbed).

Fan worm (*Myxicola infundibulum*)
If at low tide you paddle slowly in shallow, muddy water, you might be lucky enough to see *Myxicola infundibulum*, one of the beautiful fan worms that live in Percuil, where this one was photographed. You will have to be careful not to disturb it with ripples or your shadow, because it is very shy. As soon as it senses your presence it will instantaneously withdraw into its burrow. It is able to escape so quickly because it has giant nerve fibres dedicated solely to ensuring a speedy withdrawal.

Fan worms are polychaetes – marine worms with many bristles or chaetae. All you can see above the mud is the very end of its thick, gelatinous tube and its crown of tentacles, about 5 centimetres (2 inches) across. It uses its feathery crown to filter-feed on plankton drifting about in the water.

The expansive Carrick Roads, looking towards Falmouth harbour.
*St Mawes Castle is on the headland at right-hand side of the photo.**

These past searches were made in an inflatable dinghy, and followed the shoreline, so this was the first time that I had walked the path behind Place House. Thinking that it would be a tedious but necessary diversion from the shore, I was pleasantly surprised to come upon the delightful little Church of St Anthony-in-Roseland.

The Church of St Anthony-in-Roseland
The Church of St Anthony-in-Roseland is built on the same site as the former monastery, whose history is inscribed between rows of dog teeth on the south door. According to the inscriptions, Christ visited the Roseland Peninsula when his uncle Joseph of Arimathea came to trade for tin. After sheltering from a storm in the estuary, they camped at Place and left behind them a shrine, which later became the site of a very early church, then the monastery and the present church.

One of the antiquities outside the church is a moss-covered medieval stone coffin. Inside, the church is illuminated by magnificent stained-glass windows.

I was absolutely alone in the church and there was nobody in the vicinity, so I enjoyed a few minutes of quiet contemplation before leaving the church and heading to St Anthony Head.

On the way I looked out across the expansive Carrick Roads to the north-west, the docks at Falmouth, and the two castles on either side of the estuary. I attempted to photograph the scene with my little camera, but failed dismally to capture its magnificence. No camera, however sophisticated, could match being there.

Pine trees on Carricknath Point, looking towards St Anthony Head.*

I continued through the pine trees on Carricknath Point, then dropped down to a stream before climbing up to St Anthony Head and its lighthouse. One of the unusual features of the lighthouse is that, in addition to its main light, it has a red filter which warns ships when they are heading too close to the deadly Manacles. Apparently, it also has a black screen which shades the light from the residents of St Mawes.

On the way to St Anthony Head, I reminisced once again about the seashore safaris I used to make to Percuil. The sheltered muddy inlets and small coves near Place contrast sharply with the exposed rocky shores of St Anthony Head, and the even more exposed rocks of Zone Point. Here seaweeds are much less profuse and their bladders, if they have any, are much smaller. But the deep rock pools harbour animals as wonderful as those on the muddy shore. Particular favourites of mine are the prawns that you can invariably catch with a sweep or two of a pond net. Not much to look at from a distance, close-up they reveal their true splendour.

Yvonne, my sister, was waiting for me at St Anthony Head. We had planned (there's that word again) to walk part of the path together. However, the weather was turning nasty, and as Yve was with her young dogs,

Prawn (*Palaemon serratus*)
Several prawn species live in the rock pools around St Anthony Head. This is the largest. Like other decapod crustaceans, such as crabs and lobsters, it has an external skeleton and five pairs of walking legs. It uses the pincers on its front legs to search for and pick up food. Prawns hide in seaweed or move slowly over the bottom of a pool, scavenging for food. When danger threatens they quickly dart backwards.

Towan beach, with the wreck post on the left.

we decided that I should walk alone so I could keep up a quick pace. We arranged to meet again at Portloe. Taking some of my gear, Yve drove off in her four-by-four. Once again I was abandoned.

With the weather changing very quickly from dry to wet, I had no time to find the disused battery and the officers' quarters, now turned into National Trust holiday cottages. Nor was I able to look through the toposcope (viewfinder) erected on the gun apron by the National Trust. Waterproofs on, I headed south-east around Zone Point, and then down to Porthbeor beach on my way to Portscatho and Portloe.

The stretch of coast between St Anthony Head and Portscatho is easy walking, and (when dry) very pleasant. The Coast Path clings to the cliff edge for much of the way, and has the advantage of being unfenced on the landward side, making it feel very open. For a marine biologist, Porthbeor beach looked tempting, with its extensive wave-cut platform and many rock pools exposed by the low tide. But I resisted the lure of the beach, and continued around Killigerran Head.

Approaching Towan beach, I noticed a sturdy white post with climbing steps. It looked like a mast from a ship which, I found out later, is exactly what it was intended to look like. The post was a wreck post, used in the past when the Coastguard employed a breeches buoy to rescue seamen from ships in distress. The ship would fire one of Trengrouse's rockets at the pole; the rope would be made fast, and the breeches buoy brought into effect.

The word *towan* is Cornish for sand dune, so the beach must once have had dunes. The track from the beach to the car-park at Porth Farm indicates the reason for the loss. It is called a sanding road because it was once used by the farmers to bring sand and seaweed from the beach to fertilize their fields. Unfortunately, an excessive removal of sand probably resulted in destabilization of the dunes, and their subsequent erosion.

From Towan beach, I continued to follow the Coast Path along the cliff edge until I reached Portscatho. Portscatho, like most of Cornwall's

Portscatho, like most Cornish coastal towns, was formerly a pilchard-fishing village.*

coastal towns, is a former pilchard-fishing village. It has a tiny harbour which dries out at low tide. There is still some fishing for mackerel and shellfish, but most of the boats using the steep slipway nowadys are pleasure craft.

Usually, the houses of Cornish fishing villages are clustered around the harbour, but the buildings of Portscatho are spread out above the shore of a gently curving, sandy bay between reefs of grey rock. Most of the buildings are guesthouses or holiday cottages; only a few are private houses with permanent residents. One building has a particular significance for me. It is the nursing home where my mother spent her last days. It has the most amazing views across the bay to Nare Head in the distance, but I'm not sure if she was ever well enough to enjoy them.

As the tide was still out, I was able to scramble down on to Porthcurnick beach. Its acres of sand are ideal for beach games, but with the rain starting to come in there were few people in sight.

From Porthcurnick, I took the Coast Path and walked around the headland at Pednvadan, then through several fields to Porthbean beach, and from there to Pendower. Although the official path goes across the dunes, up a road and behind the Nare Hotel, I took the easier route across the beach to Carne, from where I climbed up to Nare Head.

The weather was worsening and visibility becoming poor, so I didn't linger long at Nare Head, even though it is a fine headland of exposed igneous rock from which, on a better day, you can see far inland as well as along the coast.

Leaving Nare Head and turning east, I wiped the rain from my glasses and saw Gull Rock come into view about a half mile (0.8 km) offshore. Gull Rock must be the most common name for islets around the Cornish coast.

Kittiwake (*Rissa tridactyla*)
Kittiwakes are small and elegant. Consequently, they can use tiny take-off and landing platforms. This enables them to breed in dense colonies on narrow ledges in relative safety. Kittiwakes build fairly elaborate, cup-shaped nests, using mud or their own droppings to anchor them. Sometimes a nest is so precariously positioned that only by gripping it tightly with its long, sharp claws can a kittiwake avoid falling off. Although strong in beak and claw, kittiwakes have delicate legs, not much suited to walking. This is not really surprising because kittiwakes are among the most oceanic of gulls. On breeding, adults live well out to sea and move thousands of miles from where they were raised. While at sea, they forage in flocks, capturing marine fish and invertebrates by dipping-to-surface. Adults may remain offshore for several weeks.

This one was once part of the Domesday Manor of Elerky. After only a few changes of ownership it was sold to Michael Trinick, a former Regional Director of the National Trust in Cornwall. In 1989, he gave it to the Trust to mark his appointment as High Sheriff of Cornwall. In former times, the Rock was a source of gull's eggs and even whole birds, which were used for food, but its greatest distinction came from being used as the film set for the 1950s version of *Treasure Island*. Today, no birds are caught, no eggs are taken, and no films are shot at the Rock. Its main interest is as a nesting site for seabirds. These include herring gull, guillemot, cormorant, shag and, from time to time, razorbills and fulmars. The most numerous breeding bird is the kittiwake, which takes full advantage of the near vertical, land-facing side of the rock.

Although the day had started fine, the weather was now wet, wet, wet. The path to Portloe was overgrown, and I was becoming soaked from head to toe. At times, I felt that I was wading through a river. Therefore, after slipping over a couple of stiles, I was relieved to be making a long descent to reach Portloe where Yve was waiting to pick me up.

Portloe is tucked safely between Jacka Point and Portloe Point, at the back of a narrow break in the cliffs where two valleys converge. The village is several miles from the main road, and at the end of a long stretch of narrow, winding lanes, which deters coaches and casual traffic. Combined with planning regulations that seem to be doing their job, this has resulted in a village free from the ravages of

Portloe is still a fishing village.

over-commercialization. Portloe not only looks like a fishing village, but actually functions as one, making it doubly attractive. When not at sea, boats are hauled up the slipway; the pots are stacked out of the way, and fishermen can be seen going about their business. The pace at which they do things is not the city way. Here, things are done 'dreckly'. This term has an eternal quality about it, which I have only seen matched in rural areas of South Africa where the locals do things in 'African time'.

Dripping wet, I got into Yve's four-by-four, and we splashed our way along the narrow, high-hedged lanes to her cottage at Philleigh. After soaking in a hot bath, I felt almost human again, and spent a very pleasant evening with Yve and my brother-in-law Pat. One of the most enjoyable parts of my journey was being able to stop with family and friends on the way and share my experiences with them.

Day 14 (19.5 ml/31.4 km)

Portloe to Charlestown

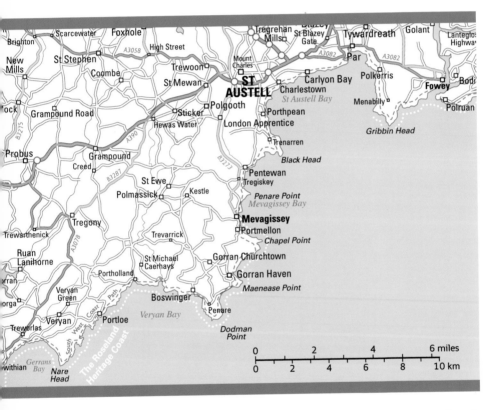

Yve returned me to Portloe just before 9 a.m. the following morning. It was still overcast, but the rain had stopped and I was able to take a photograph of the harbour.

In June, the paths were badly overgrown around Portloe, except for those managed by the National Trust. Perhaps this was another way in which the people of Portloe retained their seclusion. The damp, high vegetation made the walk out of the village extremely wet, even though it was not raining.

*Porthluney Cove.**

About a mile east of Portloe, on the cliffs at Tregenna, I encountered a group of intrepid walkers bravely sporting T-shirts and shorts. One was rattling a tin; they were on a charity walk for the Southwest Children's Hospice. After they had relieved me of some of my ill-gotten gains, I warned them about the wet vegetation ahead. One of the men replied that they'd brought the women for just such a contingency ... and sent their lady-folk ahead to blaze a trail.

From Tregenna, I descended to the twin villages and two sandy beaches of West and East Portholland, and then continued to Porthluney Cove. One feature that always makes Porthluney Cove a joy to visit is Caerhays Castle. This is such a dominant feature that we usually spoke of 'going down to Caerhays', and rarely referred to the beach as Porthluney Cove.

Caerhays Castle
The castle was built in 1808, on the site of a manor. It is famed for being designed by John Nash, the great architect who later designed the Brighton Pavilion, Buckingham Palace and Marble Arch. The castle and grounds belong to the Williams family, who open the spectacular wooded gardens between March and May each year. The gardens were originally created using specimens collected by plant hunters in China shortly after the turn of the twentieth century. Today, visitors flock from far and wide to see the magnificent magnolias, camellias and rhododendrons in full bloom. Of special interest is the *Camellia* x *williamsii*, a hybrid produced by the Castle gardeners.

The nineteenth-century cross on the Dodman – a navigational aid to mariners.

I left Caerhays by a familiar path to the east, up through a field and out on to the cliff tops. I write 'familiar' because it was along these grass-covered cliff tops that Merryn and I spent some of our courting days picnicking. As I walked towards Hemmick Beach, I noticed one small area of particularly low grass, and thought this might be the spot from where we sat to look out over Veryan Bay towards the Dodman.

Hemmick beach was another favourite haunt of ours. Even now in the height of summer, it never seems to be crowded. That's probably because access is by very narrow lanes, and there is no room behind the beach for cars. The hill to the east out of Hemmick is especially steep. So steep, in fact, that many years ago when Merryn and I tried to climb it in my old Reliant Regal (yes, I admit to starting my driving career in a fiery three-wheeler), I stalled and could only continue when Merryn got out.

In June, I didn't have to do a hill climb in a fibreglass firetrap, but I did have to scramble up the steep Coast Path to Dodman Point, more than 122 metres (400 feet) above sea level.

Cornwall's Christian heritage is well marked by many crosses that can be seen from the Coast Path. But none is any more magnificent than that at the Dodman. It was erected in 1896 by Revd G. Martin, a former rector of St Michael Caerhays, as a navigational aid to mariners. Its inscription reads, 'in the firm hope of the second coming of our Lord Jesus Christ and for the encouragement of those who strive to serve him.'

The Dodman

According to legend, the promontory acquired its name from being the final resting place of a giant. One day when this scourge of the neighbourhood fell ill, a local doctor responded to his cries for help with the advice that the giant should be bled. This was not as suspicious then as it might sound today, as bleeding was once a commonly prescribed remedy for a wide range of ills. When the loss of blood weakened the giant sufficiently, the doctor kicked him over the edge of the cliff to his death, and the promontory over which he fell became known as 'The Dead Man', or Dodman.

The Dodman is the site of probably the largest promontory fort in Cornwall. It has a huge earth rampart, known variously as the Bulwark, Baulk and the 'Hack and Cast' (pronounced locally as 'Acken Cass'). It encloses just under 20 hectares (50 acres), and is nearly 610 metres (666 yards) long and 61 metres (200 feet) from top to bottom. Nearby Bronze Age burial mounds indicate the antiquity of the Fort, but much of the earthworks was the product of an Elizabethan expansion. With the Dodman being half way along the Cornish coast it was strategically placed to keep an eye on ships during the Spanish scare of the sixteenth century.

Within the earthworks, those with a discerning eye can see the remains of a medieval strip field system, similar to the one at Willipark on the north coast.

On a path just inland from the Dodman Cross is a late eighteenth-century watch house, now set up by the National Trust as a shelter for cliff walkers. From here, an observer using a powerful telescope mounted on what is now just a rusty upright, could keep a watchful eye on ship movements in the Channel. At the threat of any danger, he would raise flags on the station's flagpole to send the appropriate signal to the Admiralty.

From the top of the Dodman, there are fantastic views up and down the coast. The sun was shining and visibility good, so I went as far out along the headland as I could safely go, and did as the *South West Coast Path Guide* suggests: I looked back towards the Lizard on triumphs past, and forward towards Rame Head and challenges still to come. Although there were still more than two days of walking to complete, I felt that the finishing tape was in sight.

From the Dodman, I continued along the Coast Path which runs above the bow-shaped beach of Vault. It started to rain, so I went quickly to Gorran Haven (page 152) – another haunt of my youth. While at university, I worked during a couple of summer holidays in a little café above the beach. The building had changed into a fish and chip shop, but when I bought myself a fry-up I was pleased to find that the standard of service was just as good as in the 1970s.

I stayed in Gorran Haven long enough to finish my meal and let the rain abate. Then I moved on towards Mevagissey via Bodrugan's Leap, Chapel Point, and Portmellon. These are all places that I know well, because for several years I lived with my sister at Kestle, a mile or so above Mevagissey. Also, when I first met Merryn she was a 'Mevagissey girl', and we spent many happy hours along this stretch of coast.

Bodrugan's Leap is the spot, just south of Chapel Point, marked on the Ordnance Survey map as Turbot Point. It was named after Sir Henry Bodrugan, who lived in the Bodrugan family's castellated manor house dur-

Gorran Haven. *

ing the reign of Henry VII. Bodrugan, when pursued by his arch enemy
Sir Richard Edgcumbe, is reputed to have leapt over the cliff and escaped
by boat to France.

Rather than detracting from its natural beauty, the houses at Chapel
Point make it appear even more striking. There are three houses, all built
between 1933 and 1938 of stone taken from the site.

I cut across the neck of Chapel Point and followed the road up to the
cliff top, where I stopped to sit on a concrete block that covered some sort
of water works. This is where I used to bring Merryn on Saturday nights
(after the *Morecambe and Wise Show*), to sit and look out across the sea to
the Eddystone Lighthouse. And to think I've been accused of not being
romantic!

From the cliff top, I made my way down into Portmellon, and walked
along the road above the beach. During high spring tides, waves commonly crash over the road. If these tides coincide with stormy weather the
road becomes impassable; in 1969, conditions were so bad that the road
was totally washed away and several nearby houses were badly damaged. However, when conditions are less hostile, cars are tempted to beat
the waves and try to get from one side to the other. One popular pastime
among locals was to sit on the wall near the Rising Sun Inn and specu-
late as to which of the cars daring to make the run along the road would
be successful. Timing was of the essence. If correct, it was possible to
complete the run between waves and reach the other side unscathed. If
timing was off, even by a split second, cars would become flooded with
salty water, stall and require assistance, usually from the local garage.

Looking back from Mevagissey to Chapel Point. *

To be fair to us, we used to warn oncomers of the impending risks, but such warnings were rarely heeded.

Although Portmellon was in the past distinct from Mevagissey, known for its boat-building rather than fishing, today it merges with Mevagissey, which was my next port of call.

When I was a boy, Mevagissey was known as 'Fishygissey', because of the smells emanating from fish processing. Added to these odours was the stench from its Victorian sewage system. This has since been modernized, and the area around the harbour has a more pleasant aroma.

Mevagissey is now dependent on the holiday trade, but it was once one of the most important fishing ports in Cornwall. In its early days, the main catch was pilchard. Sometimes catches were so great that the whole village reeked of fish. Up to the end of the nineteenth century it supplied pilchard to the Royal Navy, which called the fish 'Mevagissey duck'. There was an attempt to revive the pilchard fishery in the 1950s, but it was not successful.

I tend to associate Mevagissey with mackerel, partly because I used to angle for this fish off the outer harbour. It is also the fish that became increasingly important when pilchard stocks declined.

Mackerel

One look at a mackerel leaves you in no doubt as to what it is and what it does. It is an exemplary fish, ideally suited to its free-swimming, predatory mode of life. Beautifully coloured, and counter-shaded for concealment in the upper, sunlit layers of the sea, its powerful muscles and exquisitely streamlined shape enable it to move quickly and with apparent ease through the water. Mackerel are seasonal migrants. Those that I used to catch in the outer harbour had come inshore to feed off zooplankton and fish fry. In the winter, mackerel go into deeper water. Around the Cornish coast, there are about 150 vessels that fish commercially for mackerel. The largest vessels are based at Newlyn, Mevagissey and Looe.

Pentewan beach, and caravans at Pentewan Sands Holiday Park. *

I exited Mevagissey by climbing the path on the north side of the inner harbour, past some pretty little cottages of the former Coastguard Station. When I reached the open space on the cliff top, I headed for the Coast Path to Pentewan. Although I've done it many times, it always surprises me how tough the walk is between Mevagissey and Pentewan. Eventually, after a series of steep ups and downs, Pentewan sands, backed by a neat array of caravans, came into sight. Just offshore was what appeared to be some sort of large landing craft.

I crossed the beach, and then looked at the White River, which flows from the moorlands above St Austell down through Pentewan valley and on to the beach. The White River is, at most, just a few metres wide, so it's more of a stream than a river. Neither is it white. It now flows clear enough to allow freshwater plants to grow. But the White River got its name because it was fed from water coming from clay-mining areas. Then it ran as milky as white emulsion, due to the very fine particles of white kaolin it carried.

After crossing the beach and walking through the village, I climbed Pentewan Hill and rejoined the Coast Path, which took me towards Black Head on my way to Porthpean.

As a teenager, I often went out to Black Head with a friend in a double-seated kayak to search for marine creatures. It was such trips that sparked my interest in marine biology. I remember that the deep, calm pools with a good growth of kelp (the large brown weeds found at the low-tide mark) were particularly good places to find sea urchins, starfish and edible crabs. But in June, having no kayak to help explore the shallows around Black Head, I cut across its neck and continued along the cliff path above Ropehaven.

Sea urchin (*Echinus esculentus*)
(Photographed in Blue Reef Aquarium Newquay, in the arms of a brittlestar.) Sea urchins are echinoderms – marine animals with spiny skins. The body of a sea urchin, like that of the common starfish, is divided into five parts. It moves by means of water-filled, translucent tube feet, arranged in five radiating bands on its test, or shell. Like a starfish, a sea urchin has its mouth centrally placed on its undersurface. Look into its mouth and you will see the tips of its five white, pointed teeth, with which it crunches kelp and grazes on the animals attached to the kelp's surface. The spines of the common sea urchin are short, sharp and violet-tipped. They cover the test thickly and evenly. Among them are smaller structures bearing tweezer-like jaws on flexible stalks. These are called pedicellariae, and are used to groom the surface of the test clean. One type of pedicellaria is associated with toxin-secreting cells. These probably have an anti-fouling function, preventing algae and fungi from settling on the test; they are not known to cause any harm to a person handling sea urchins.

On the way to Porthpean, I had good views across St Austell Bay, and inland to the town where I spent nearly all of my childhood. Rising above the town, I could see the granite moors of Hensbarrow and its china clay tips, only a few of which still have the shape which earned them the name 'white pyramids' (page 156).

When I arrived at Porthpean, the tide was in. It was evening, and there were few people on the beach. I lingered at the top of the slipway, and looked out across the beach to what we used to call Gull Rock to the north, and Robins Rock to the south. It was on this beach that I spent most of my teenage summers, swimming, snorkelling,

Starfish (*Asterias rubens*)
The starfish, or sea star, is unmistakable, with its five arms and rows of tube feet on the underside. The feet help it to move slowly over the sea floor, and let it attach itself to rocks, making it difficult for predators to remove it. The mouth is in the centre of the body, also on the underside, and the starfish can push its stomach out through the mouth to digest its prey. It feeds on mussels, worms, crustaceans and echinoderms.

kayaking and playing beach games. It is also the beach that I came to know best in terms of its marine life. For several years, I would visit it once every week or two, and search among the rocks, pools and seaweed for their treasures of marine nature. It was here that I first saw all sorts of weird and wonderful creatures. There were permanent residents, such

The view from Trenarren to Porthpean. A china-clay tip, or 'white pyramid' is in the distance, on the left of the photo.

Kaolin, or china clay

Ever since their formation some 300 million years ago, the moors of Hensbarrow have undergone a complex series of changes. The constant circulation of water over many millions of years, and the repeated dissolution and recrystallization of minerals, has altered the granite from being a hard rock into soft china clay.

It was William Cookworthy who, in 1748, first discovered china clay deposits at Hensbarrow and developed china-clay mining as a new industry. For more than 200 years, the industry flourished, with Charlestown, Par and Fowey being the major ports from which china clay was exported.

Originally, the china clay was used mainly to produce excellent white china for potters such as Josiah Wedgwood. Today, it is used in innumerable products, including paper, medicines, paints and soap, as well as pots.

Hensbarrow was the most important area for china clay extraction, but deposits have also been exploited on Bodmin Moor and at Lee Moor, on the south-western part of Dartmoor.

If West Cornwall has been built on tin and copper, St Austell and its surrounding villages have been built on kaolin. Colin Bristow, who joined English China Clays in 1962 as a geologist, and became Visiting Professor in Industrial Geology at the Camborne School of Mines, estimated the total production values (at 2003 prices) of all minerals that have been extracted from the Cornubian orefield (this includes the whole of Cornwall and those mineralized areas associated with Dartmoor granite). The value of china clay came out top at £13,600 million, with tin a distant second at £4,800 million (C.M. Bristow, *Cornwall's Geology and Scenery*, 2004). No wonder kaolin has been called 'white gold'.

There are still significant deposits of china clay at Hensbarrow, but with deposits elsewhere in the world cheaper to extract, the industry is in serious decline. Tourism – a different form of 'extractive' industry – appears to be taking its place, as indicated by the development of The Eden Project in a former china clay pit just outside St Austell.

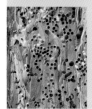

Mermaid's purse, goose barnacle and shipworm

Mermaid's purses (top) are the egg cases of dogfish, skates and rays. When found on the shore they are usually dried out, horny and empty. Those containing young fish are more translucent; you can sometimes see the developing embryo attached to its yolk sac.

Goose barnacles (*Lepas* sp., middle) are also called stalked barnacles, or ship's barnacles. They are filter-feeding crustaceans (the group to which crabs, lobsters and shrimps belong), and are closely related to acorn barnacles (the very common small type found on most intertidal rocks). Goose barnacles are cast ashore at irregular intervals, usually on pieces of wood, but sometimes on other objects such as sandals or even balls of tar. They gained their common name because their fleshy stalk and shell resemble a goose's neck, and their feathery appendages a goose's wings, leading to the myth that the barnacles grew up and turned into barnacle geese. It is said that in the past some Catholics used this belief to justify eating barnacle geese on religious days, when meat other than seafood was banned.

Shipworm is not a worm at all, but a bivalve mollusc. It uses its two shells to gouge out tunnels a few millimetres in diameter in sea-soaked wood (bottom). Many untreated ships and piers have been destroyed by the activities of shipworm, ending up as pieces of wood drifting the oceans.

as gobies, blennies and rocklings; local visitors, such as fish fry stranded temporarily in a tide pool, or starfish and mermaid's purses thrown on to the beach after a storm; and exotic visitors which came drifting in on currents from the faraway tropics. The latter included the venomous jellyfish-like Portugese-man-of-war, which came on its own float; goose barnacles attached to driftwood, and shipworms hiding within a piece of wooden wreckage.

I left Porthpean knowing that it would not be long before I would return to this favourite haunt of my youth. I climbed the many steps to the top of the cliff on the north side of the beach; walked past the two-storey Second World War lookout tower (the site of many childhood games), and headed towards Duporth.

I was stopped in my tracks by a fence, in front of which was a sign informing me that the Coast Path was closed because of a cliff fall. I looked over the fence, and could see that in the several years since I had walked this stretch of Coast Path, the cliffs had receded to the very edge of the gardens of the Duporth houses. There was no alternative but to follow the diversion up Porthpean hill, along Porthpean Road, down through the woods of Duporth and into Charlestown. This really was a walk down memory lane, for I used to live just off Porthpean Road in Mount Charles, and I must have done the walk hundreds of times in the past. With my mind going through a series of flashbacks as I walked past particularly significant spots, before I realized it I had reached Charlestown where Merryn was waiting to take me home for the night.

Day 15 (22.4 ml/36.1 km)

Charlestown
to Looe

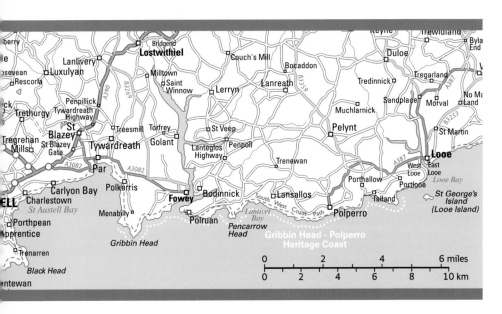

On Sunday morning, Merryn and I returned to Charlestown where for the third and last time she abandoned me, to complete the walk on my own.

Charlestown, with a tall ship moored in the harbour, was looking splendid in the early morning sun. The ship is one of a fleet belonging to Square Sail, the company which also owns the harbour and the two beaches on either side of it.

Going down to the harbour and on to the beaches brought back many memories. In the 1950s, during the early years of my childhood, it was to Charlestown and its main beach that we would most often walk. And it was at low tide, in the pool behind the small breakwater, that I first learned to swim, aided by threats from my two older sisters.

I remember that at this time Charlestown was still a very busy port. At each tide, more than a dozen heavy transport lorries would queue along the road above the east side of the harbour, and wait their turn to unload tonnes of china clay down the steep chutes into waiting ships.

Charlestown, a Georgian 'new town'. The harbour is home to many old ships, and has been the setting for numerous films.*

Charlestown

Charlestown originated as a small settlement called West Polmeor. In 1790 it had a population of just nine people. The population, along with its name, changed in 1801 when Charles Rashleigh built a harbour for ships to take away china clay, tin and copper, and to bring in coke and coal. At its peak, in the early part of the twentieth century, Charlestown had a population of well over 3,000. It was a very busy port, with the reputation of being dirty. Folliott-Stokes wrote in *The Cornish Coast and Moors* that Charlestown should change its name to Little Hades, because

> The smoke of its torment ascended in heavy clouds of black and white dust as we scrambled down the steep hill-side into the gruesome pit, where a crowd of undistinguished beings are for ever emptying and loading an inexhaustible fleet of schooners. What the natural features of Charlestown originally were it is impossible to say, for everything is coated with white or black dust, and sometimes with both together, the result being a most depressing grey, as of ashes.

And he didn't even mention the gobs of black tar that invariably stuck to the feet after a visit to the beach.

In the 1960s Charlestown began to decline, along with the china clay industry. Houses were grubby from accumulated dust, and the whole place looked a bit run down. But Charlestown had a complete makeover for the 1976 film *The Eagle Has Landed* – a Second World War drama starring Michael Caine, Donald Sutherland, Jenny Agutter and Robert Duval. Television aerials were removed; a 'gun' sited near the harbour, and the houses redecorated to fit the 1940s scenario. The film led to the village becoming much better known. With its newly painted Georgian houses, it soon developed into a very desirable place in which to live, as it continues to be today.

*The beach at Crinnis, where the Cornish Riviera Lido was being pulled down.**

Charlestown's pebbled beach
Most of the pebbles on the beach to the east of Charlestown harbour are not of local origin. They are the ballast from otherwise un-laden vessels making their way to Charlestown from foreign ports. The ballast would have been unloaded before taking in the cargo of china clay or, in earlier days, tin and copper.

After a brief walk reminiscing, I rejoined the Coast Path and made my way to Carlyon Bay.

The beach at Crinnis looked as if several bombs had hit it. The large building which I had known as the Cornish Riviera Lido was being pulled down, and the ground around it prepared for a major new development. There are plans to build a luxury holiday village on the beach, with 500 plush apartments, but these plans are being opposed by a local residents' group. Those in favour of the development argue that the beach is a brown-field site that has already been developed, and the construction of high-quality holiday properties would greatly benefit the local economy. Those against argue that it would severely limit access to a very popular beach, and spoil its natural beauty. At the time of writing, planning permission for an already partially constructed sea wall has been refused, and there is much uncertainty about the future of the development.

I peered through the fence at Crinnis, and continued along the Coast Path on the cliff tops beside the Carlyon Bay Golf Club to Spit Point.

The walk between Spit and Par beach is not the prettiest. Part of it is through highly fenced paths next to Par harbour. Unattractive china-clay installations dominate the scene, but these were all part of the paraphernalia which brought jobs and wealth to St Austell. I say 'were' because, although the buildings are still present and smoke still billows out of the chimneys of the china-clay driers, the industrial activity is much reduced.

Par beach, looking west towards the harbour and china-clay installations.

From Spit and the entrance to Par harbour, I walked along the road into Par. The official Coast Path goes through the village along Par Green, and past the Welcome Inn to the alms houses at Polmear, but I decided to go on to the beach before rejoining the Coast Path.

Par beach has a split personality. Its western side is dominated by the harbour and its industrial complex of mineral grinding and drying plants, and storage tanks. Its eastern side is much more serene, with few buildings spoiling the natural beauty of its cliffs and fields.

Par harbour

Par harbour was constructed by Joseph Julian Treffry between 1829 and 1841. Treffry was a mining magnate and adventurer who became known as the 'King of mid-Cornwall', for his power and influence in the area. He owned granite quarries and china-clay workings, and it was he who built the famous viaduct across the Luxulyan valley. To make the harbour, Treffry enclosed 14 hectares (35 acres) of water with a breakwater 366 metres (1,200 feet) long. He also had to remove tons of silt that had accumulated in the mouth of Par River before he could install the extensive harbour works. At one time, Par was one of the busiest small ports in the world. When completed, the port could accommodate 50 vessels of 180 tonnes (200 tons). In 1987 it handled over 635,000 tonnes (700,000 tons) of china clay. In recent years, the traffic has declined so much that, according to a report on the BBC news on 6 July 2007, the port was to close by the end of the year, and would no longer be used by ships exporting china clay.

(Indeed, from January 2008, the china-clay business was transferred to Fowey, whose harbour can accommodate larger vessels. The long-term future of the docks at Par was still under discussion, with the possibility that they would remain open for other business.)

Razor shell (*Ensis* sp.)
Razor shells, named because their shells are similar to old-fashioned cut-throat razors, are bivalve molluscs. They live in sand towards the low-tide mark, in deep, vertical, semi-permanent burrows. When covered by the sea, they move towards the top of the burrow to feed and respire. If disturbed, they retreat quickly down into the sand, using their powerful, muscular foot. A razor shell removed from its burrow and placed on damp sand will hook its foot into the sand, and use its muscles to pull its shell vertically downwards, completely burying itself in a matter of seconds. A razor shell leaves a characteristic key-hole depression when it burrows into the sand. Those collecting the mollusc to make a meal out of its meaty tissue often use the simple trick of tipping table salt into the depression. This causes the bivalve to reappear at the surface. Empty shells are often found stranded towards the high-tide mark after being carried up the shore by an incoming tide.

When Folliott-Stokes came to Par and St Blazey, he wrote that they 'possess no attractions worth turning aside to see...', but when I was a boy, Par was a place of great excitement, for it was where we came to have our holidays. Although our home in St Austell was only five or six miles away, Par with its marshes, sand dunes, cliffs and sea was a world away.

We hired a couple of beach huts or a caravan for a week or two, and spent from dawn to dusk messing about on the beach, or paddling boats on the lake. One of my pleasures was to search for seashells on the sands on a low spring tide. The beach has a very shallow gradient, so the tide goes out for up to a half a mile, exposing a huge area of sand – probably the most extensive on the coast of South Cornwall. Among my most common finds were elongated razor shells. Today, razor shells and other seashells can still be found on the beach, but the huts have gone. And, although there are still plenty of caravans, Par is not the major tourist site it once was.

To rejoin the Coast Path, I clambered up the rocks to the top of the cliffs at Polmear, on the eastern side of Par beach. From here, I walked via Polkerris around Gribbin Head to Polridmouth, and then on to Fowey.

Polkerris is a semicircular, sandy cove, protected on its southern flank by a stone jetty, and on its northern flank by rocks. The castle-like structure at the back of the beach is the now defunct pilchard cellar constructed in Tudor times. The cellar was one of the longest in Cornwall. Millions of fish have been packed within its walls, and thousands of gallons of oil have oozed out from the barrels being pressed. Today, there's not even a whiff of fish – except perhaps the appetizing smell of those being served in the nearby Rashleigh Arms. Polkerris has been referred to as one of Cornwall's most perfect fishing villages. Thankfully, with only a public

The semicircular cove at Polkerris, protected from the sea by its stone jetty. *

house, café, and a few straggling cottages, the village has avoided over-commercialization.

I left Polkerris by taking the zig-zag path through the sycamore woods, and then headed for the daymark at Gribbin Head.

The daymark at Gribbin Head

The red-and-white, candy-striped 26-metre (84-foot) daymark makes the Gribbin instantly recognizable. The daymark was erected in 1832 by Trinity House, so mariners could identify the approaches to Fowey Harbour, and to distinguish the Gribbin from similar-looking headlands near Falmouth. The daymark is now owned by the National Trust, which opens it on several days in the summer to allow visitors to climb to the top and admire the magnificent views across the Bay.

Polridmouth, and part of the Menabilly estate.*

From the Gribbin, I walked down to Polridmouth (usually shortened to Pridmouth), the cove below Menabilly. The delightful house at the back of the beach and next to a lake is the dwelling that gave Daphne du Maurier the inspiration for her romantic novel, *Rebecca*. Manderley, the house which features so strongly in the book, is based on Menabilly House, about half a mile up the valley. Menabilliy House was the seat of the Rashleigh family for 400 years. Daphne du Maurier lived there herself for several years.

After making my way across the concrete path and stones by the beach house, I continued along the Coast Path above two small coves, and then through Covington Woods. At the bottom of the woods the Coast Path crosses another long-distance path, the Saints Way, marked with its own unique symbol of a stylized Celtic cross. Opened in May 1986, the Saints Way is a modern reconstruction of one of the Dark Age (AD 400–700) routes by which Celtic monks and merchants made their way between Fowey and Padstow.

Bearing left at the bottom of the woods, I went to Readymoney Cove and then into Fowey. In the Middle Ages, Fowey's deep-water inlet and easily defended narrow entrance made it the premier port of Cornwall. It was the home of the Fowey Gallants – daring and dastardly seamen who built an infamous reputation as privateers. There are many stories about their skirmishes. They sent 47 ships and 770 men to Edward III's siege of Calais. When Edward IV made peace with France, the Gallants continued

Looking down to Fowey harbour. Place House, home of the Treffry family, is on the left, and the parish church of St Fimbarrus on the right.

the war on their own. It is not surprising that in 1457 the French took revenge by raiding Fowey. Although the raid was beaten off, much of Fowey was burnt. But despite French attempts to destroy it, Fowey recovered. With its large ships carrying china clay to destinations all over the world, it is still an active port today, but nothing like its glory days during the swashbuckling Middle Ages.

Fowey is another of my favourite places. As an undergraduate, I spent a summer kayaking into its sinuous, wood-lined creeks to study the ragworms and lugworms living there. For three years during my PhD research into a shellfish pest, I visited Fowey once a fortnight and walked from the wharves north of the town all the way up to Lostwithiel via Golant. I came to know this unique estuary very well. Its harmonious blend of history and modernity; its beautiful compactness; its fantastic scenery and wonderful wildlife enchanted me. But on the fifteenth day of my walk around Cornwall there was no time for an estuarine excursion, and I pressed on to Polruan via the foot ferry that left from the quay.

At Polruan, I recharged with a pint and a pasty, and then walked up the hill to find the Coast Path. After a couple of wrong turnings, I found myself on a clear path to Polperro. With Polruan behind me, I faced what is probably the toughest stretch of walking on the South Cornwall coast.

I walked quickly to Blackbottle Rock, paused there to take advantage of the views along the coast, then continued above Lantic Bay to Pencarrow Head, where Dexter cattle and Dartmoor ponies help to restrict the growth of scrub and encourage wildflowers. Just beyond the headland, I

Thrift clearwing (*Synansphecia [=Bembecia] muscaeformis*)
This little moth was caught with a pheromone lure at Pencarrow Head. With a wingspan of only 16–20 mm (0.5–0.75 inch), it is the smallest of our native clearwings. Although rarely seen, it is quite common on the sea cliffs and rocky coasts of western England, Wales and parts of Scotland, where its food-plant occurs. These moths are active during daylight, and can be found visiting the flowers of thyme (*Thymus*) as well as thrift. The food plant of the caterpillars is thrift (*Armeria maritima*). The larvae feed in the roots and crown of the plant, seeming to prefer smaller plants growing on bare rock to large clumps. The moths overwinter as larvae, which betray their presence by a small, reddish patch on the cushion of the plant.

met John Nicholls, a member of the Caradon Natural History Society. He was carrying out a survey of a maritime moth called the thrift clearwing. Because of its small size and good camouflage, this moth usually goes unnoticed by the casual observer. But John had a devious device for luring the moths into a trap, which involved soaking cotton wool with pheromones (chemicals that a female oozes in order to attract a mate). By this means, John had found 21 moths on the headland.

When John had finished explaining to me what he was doing, I continued eastwards along the Coast Path to West Coombe. Just inland of West Coombe is the fifteenth-century church of St Ildierna at Lansallos. I did not follow the track that leads to it, but pressed on through National Trust land to Polperro, on the way passing the white-painted navigation aid marking the Udder Rock.

Polperro is at the end of a river valley, which in the past made it liable to flooding. In 1976, a cloudburst swept down the valley and devastated the village. A new defence scheme was installed, which should prevent this from happening again.

Polperro village consists of a huddle of buildings tucked snugly under lofty hills. It is very picturesque, with some quaint cottages and houses. One, covered with thousands of different sea shells, is particularly eye-catching. Another is the cottage in which one of my Cornish heroes, Jonathan Couch (page 168), lived in the nineteenth century. He was an extraordinarily gifted naturalist who contributed much to our understanding of Cornish wildlife.

As would be expected from its position, Polperro has a long history of smuggling, fishing and seafaring. All these attractions bring many visitors, and in summer Polperro's narrow streets are crammed.

After crossing the Roman bridge I took the path out of Polperro, stopping to look at the harbour. It is almost landlocked, with an entrance guarded by slaty outcrops only a few metres apart. Despite its sheltered position, Polperro has not escaped the ravages of violent seas.

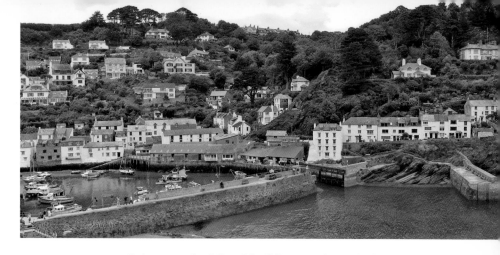

Polperro, a huddle of buildings at the end of a river valley, has a long history of smuggling, fishing and seafaring.*

Thirty vessels were destroyed there in 1817, and the pier has been severely damaged on other occasions. From my vantage point on the Coast Path, I could see much activity as small boats laden with pots entered the harbour. I was delighted to read that the harbour was a self-supporting enterprise, maintained as an active fishing port by Trustees. I read their information sign, which stated that they were '... anxious to maintain it without further commercialisation'; made a modest contribution to the help they were seeking, and left Polperro to head for Looe.

I passed the spectacularly sited War Memorial on Downend Point, and continued east. On my way, I noticed two pairs of black-and-white striped beacons, set some distance apart. I found out later that they delineate a measured nautical mile for speed trials offshore. Progressing slower than a boat to China, and needing a calendar rather than a watch to time my passage, I was pleased no one was measuring my speed.

A house at Polperro covered with sea shells. Polperro has many pretty places, but none is more flamboyant and eye-catching than this house covered in shells.

Couch's House stands next to the stream that flows through Polperro.

Dr Jonathan Couch (1789 –1870)

Jonathan Couch is probably the most famous son of Polperro. He was schooled in Cornwall, and studied medicine in London, returning as a doctor in 1810.

Jonathan Couch's many interests included archaeology, religion, the classics and local history. His book *A History of Polperro* was published in 1871 by his son, Thomas Quiller Couch. He is probably best known as a prodigiously talented zoologist who made major contributions to natural history, and particularly to our understanding of Cornwall's wildlife. In addition to compiling 12 volumes of a *Journal of Natural History*, a *Cornish Fauna* and a study of Cornish birds, he wrote *A History of the Fishes of the British Isles*, published in 1864 in four volumes. Wonderfully illustrated with 259 colour plates based on Couch's drawings, it is a classic still used by zoologists today. Many of the fish illustrated were brought to Jonathan Couch by Polperro fishermen. Apparently he kept them immersed in water in order to preserve their colours while he drew them. Copies of some of his drawings are displayed at the Polperro Heritage Museum. After he died, his grandson, Sir Arthur Quiller-Couch (the scholar, writer and compiler of the enormously successful *Oxford Book of English Verse*) described him as 'a patient man of science who spent his life observing the habits of fish, without attempting to teach the Almighty how to improve them.'

After skirting Talland Bay and rounding the point called Hore Stone, St George's Island (or Looe Island) came into view.

I continued all the way to Hannafore along the path that hugs the coastline. Unable to find any accommodation there, I went into West Looe, where I obtained a very pleasant room for the night, overlooking the river. I bought myself something to eat and, having walked about 22 miles (35 km) during the day, I was ready for bed, even though it was only 9 p.m.

St George's Island, or Looe Island, is managed by the Cornwall Wildlife Trust as part of the Looe Voluntary Conservation Area.

St George's Island (Looe Island)

St George's Island is now part of the Looe Voluntary Conservation Area, and is managed by CWT. In the 1960s, two sisters from Surrey acquired the island, intent on caring for its wildlife. (Their story was told by one of them, Evelyn Atkins, in two books, *We bought an Island* and *Tales from our Cornish Island*.) In 2000, after the death of her sister, Babs Atkins leased the island to CWT, and when she died four years later she left it to the Trust, which continues to manage it as a nature reserve.

It is one of only a few inhabited islands off the coast of Cornwall. Considering its relatively small size, it has a variety of habitats including woodland, maritime grassland, cliffs, and shores of sand, shingle and rock. Its woods are resplendent with wild garlic and bluebells in the spring. This is the time of year that large black-backed gulls come to nest on the cliffs. The nearby sea teems with marine life, with dolphins, grey seals and even basking sharks frequently seen on its surface. People lived on the island at least as far back as 1139, when a Benedictine chapel was built on its highest point. A few stones can still be seen on the original site. Since then, a small number of people have lived on the island. They have survived mainly by farming its 9 hectares (22 acres), and fishing in the local waters. There are rumours that incomes were supplemented by smuggling, but this would have been difficult after the main house was built by HM Customs to keep an eye on such illegal activities around Looe and Talland Bay. Between Easter and September it is possible to get a boat from East Looe and visit the Island, which is still home to a number of people.

Day 16 (20.9 ml/33.6 km)

Looe to Cremyll

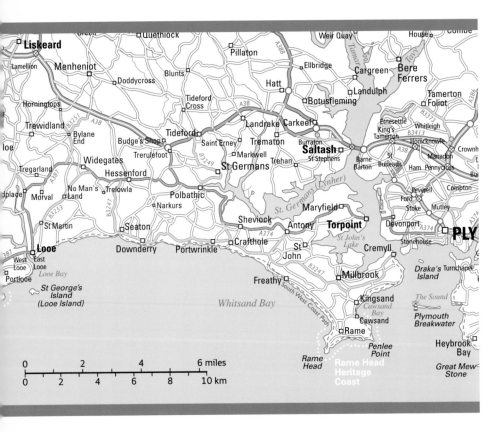

The sixteenth and final day of my walk started much as the first had done – drizzly and wet. Keen to get underway, I left my overnight accommodation just before 6 a.m., made my way through West Looe, and crossed the bridge to East Looe.

Until 1832, East and West Looe were two separate fishing communities. Both had been granted Charters in the thirteenth century. Early morning, before the streets become crowded, is a good time to see them.

West and East Looe, and the nineteenth-century bridge that links them. *

The arched bridge that links the two sides was built in 1853, replacing a fifteenth-century bridge that was too narrow for nineteenth-century traffic. Here, I paused to look down the valley at the boats moored in the harbour, and up the valley to the ancient oak woodland of Kilminorth Woods, which lines West Looe River. At spring high tide, water rises so high that it almost touches the tips of the branches.

From the car-park in West Looe, not far upstream from the bridge, there is a splendid view of an active heronry. At low tide, especially early in the morning, adult grey herons (*Ardea cinerea*) can often be seen feeding in the muddy creek in front of the car-park. This is my favourite bird. I love to watch it standing perfectly balanced on one leg, and then skilfully spear its prey – usually a small fish, but sometimes a frog or beetle. It is even known to take rats and small birds.

Looe has been described as 'a commercialized idea of a "genuine" Cornish fishing village'. This is a bit unfair. Although many of its shops, cafés and restaurants are designed to encourage tourists to spend their hard-earned cash, the town still has an active fishing fleet. It has more than a dozen otter trawlers of 9–15 metres (30–50 feet), 20 or so smaller boats that use nets and hand-lines, and about 10 boats that work part-time, mainly

Grey heron feeding in a creek. Adrian Langdon's photo sequence captures the intense concentration of a heron as it stealthily stalks its prey.

using hand-lines to fish for mackerel. The larger boats fish up to 40 miles (64 km) out to sea, but the majority of fishing takes place no more than 12 miles (20 km) off the coast, between the Eddystone Lighthouse and the Lizard. During late autumn and winter, cod, lemon sole and whiting make up most of the catch. In spring and summer, flatfish, squid and cuttlefish are more important. Looe is also a centre for angling tourism, and several boats offer charter trips out to local wrecks to fish for blue shark and mackerel.

Not seduced by the wares in the few shops that were open early in the morning, I departed from East Looe. Like many areas close to a town, this was not the easiest part of the Coast Path to navigate, and as the rain was starting to pour down, it was not the prettiest. Nevertheless, by turning up Castle Street, going up a hill and continuing along roads and tarmac paths, I found I was heading in the direction of Seaton.

Making my way towards Plaidy Beach, I thought I saw a fulmar. Despite the poor visibility, made more difficult by my glasses steaming up, I'm fairly sure of my identification. In typical fulmar fashion, it was flying low across the waves with wings stiff, except for the occasional flap, and it demonstrated its exceptional flying ability by using an up-current to move with great precision close to a cliff face. These fine seabirds – relatives of the albatross – can be seen on many stretches of the Cornish coast, and they are known to perch on the rocky outcrop to the south of Plaidy Beach.

I didn't stop at Plaidy Beach, nor at the next beach below the village of Millendreath. They are pleasant enough, but in wet weather they had nothing special to detain me.

I continued from Millendreath towards Seaton. The Coast Path

Fulmar (*Fulmarus glacialis*)
Because of its plumage pattern, a fulmar is sometimes mistaken for a gull, but it belongs to a group that includes the petrel, shearwater and albatross. Unlike gulls, all of these have tubular nostrils. The fulmar's double-tubed nostrils have been linked to the bird's exceptional sense of smell, and its ability to gauge its own speed when in flight, but their functions are still much debated.

Until 1878, British fulmar colonies were confined to St Kilda. Since then, the species has spread widely, breeding all around Britain. Cornish nesting sites include the high ledges on the cliffs between Port Isaac and Pentire Point, Ropehaven in St Austell Bay, and the rocky outcrop south of Plaidy Beach. If a nesting bird is disturbed by a predator or an over-inquisitive bird-watcher, the fulmar projects a jet of evil-smelling, oily liquid over the intruder – a sure sign that it wants to be left in peace. Clumsy and feeble on land, a fulmar has extraordinary powers of flight. It is extremely agile in the air – able to twist and turn with precision close to cliffs, even in very strong winds.

*High tide at Downderry.**

goes through Bodigga Cliff – at 155 metres (508 feet) the highest point on the south coast. The area is owned by the National Trust, and the well-managed paths have been designed to allow wheel-chair access to this popular picnic spot. From Bodigga Cliff, I passed through Bucklawren Woods. Its information board boasted of deer, foxes and badgers, but I saw none – I think that they had the good sense to lie low on such a wet and dreary day. After emerging from the woods and going through some scrubby land, I eventually reached the main road that took me into Seaton.

It was about 8 a.m. when I arrived at Seaton. The holiday camp behind the beach had not yet woken up. The only signs of activity were reluctant pupils making somnolent efforts to catch the school bus.

From Seaton, I walked to Downderry, a half a mile (0.8 km) or so further east. I would have preferred to have gone along the beach, but the tide was in so I had to risk taking the narrow, busy road.

At Downderry, I bought food in a small shop, and then took the road opposite the Methodist church that leads down to the beach. This was yet another walk down memory lane. A quarter of a century ago (was it really that long?), I lived in Mount House, a three-storey building next to the Methodist church. I walked the beach of silvery sand and shingle most days, winter and summer. Today, apart from me, there was only a lone walker and his dog braving the elements.

I finished my impromptu breakfast, and after a few moments of nostalgia continued my journey. I rejoined the official route which took me out of Downderry, up a winding path, through a field, and along the top of Battern Cliffs to Portwrinkle.

The grey-sand beach and harbour at Portwrinkle.*

Portwrinkle consists of a small beach of greyish sand, hemmed in by rocks, and a cove sheltered by a stone quay. Like so many such places, it is a former pilchard-fishing port. The buildings at the top of the slip above the harbour were pilchard cellars. The recesses in the two white-painted stone plinths on the hillside to the west of the village had fires lit in them to guide boats back to the cove after dark.

Portwrinkle is no longer a pilchard-fishing port, but it is a base for inshore crabbers. In spring and summer, pots are set near the hiding places and feeding grounds of lobsters and large edible crabs. Restaurants and hotels in Looe and the surrounding area provide a ready market for the catches. When not dealing with pots, these small boats, easily identified by the small mizzen mast offset to the port side, are usually hauled up to the top of the beach and protected by the stone quay.

From Portwrinkle harbour, I walked east along the road past the car-park, and rejoined the Coast Path opposite the Whitsand Bay Hotel. The path continues to the Golf Course, and along its edge to Trethill Cliffs. On my way, I took great care to heed the advice of the sign which said 'Beware! Falling golf balls. Keep to public footpath.'

After entering the National Trust land at Trethill Cliff, I headed for Tregantle. Nearing the fort, I saw a red flag warning that the firing range was in use. This was soon confirmed by the sound of gunshots. I had to take the official route out on to the busy B3247. I have to say that this stretch was more dangerous than walking the crumbling cliffs near the Lizard, or the rocky outcrops around Zennor. It was even more hazardous than being on the Golf Course. On one short stretch of the B3247, cars and lorries whizzed past, as if trying to see how close they could get without actually hitting me. Thankfully, I soon reached a wide grass verge, and made my way safely around Tregantle Fort, a barracks built as a national monument after the Napoleonic wars.

Lobster (*Homarus gammarus*)
It is a surprise to many people who have only seen a lobster served as a thermidore to find that in life it is mainly a beautiful dark blue colour, with pale yellow markings. Although its long antennae are red, it's only after cooking that the remainder of its body armour goes a similar colour. Although you can very occasionally find a lobster in deep, intertidal crevices near a permanent rock pool, most live below the tidemarks. Like edible crabs, they tend to shift inshore in spring and summer, and move out into deeper water in the winter. Apart from coming together to mate, lobsters are solitary crustaceans, with a reputation for aggression and cannibalism.

A lobster has two powerful claws that usually differ in size, shape and function. One – most commonly the right – is bigger and heavier, and has blunt teeth for crushing. The other is smaller, more slender and sharper, and has fine teeth for cutting. A lobster sometimes holds its prey with the cutting claw, and then administers a crushing blow with its heavier claw. Indeed, when a diver probes an arm into an occupied crevice, the lobster lodging there may treat the intruding hand in a similar fashion. Lobster claws are high-performance structures. They can produce the strongest force exerted by any animal, for a given weight, and it is best to handle them with the respect they deserve.

Before a freshly caught live lobster is placed in a holding tank, each claw is tightly bound to prevent it from damaging other lobsters.

From here, I turned right and walked down the road leading to Freathy car-park. As the tide was in there was little point in going down on to the sands, so I kept to the road for another couple of miles. Then I veered right to get on to the path that leads to Polhawn Fort and Rame Head.

For more than four miles (6.4 km), I had been walking mainly on the road, rather than on a path or track. That is usually the

Looking back along the coast to Freathy.

cause of much moaning, but this road is different. Being on the top of 76-metre (250-foot) cliffs, and with great views along a straight stretch of coast that extends from Tregantle almost to Polhawn Cove, this must

Whitsand Bay, looking west.*

be one of the most scenic roads in Cornwall. It doesn't matter if you are travelling by Shanks's pony or motorized transport, the views are glorious. Walking has the advantage of keeping you in touch with the elements. Feeling the wind against your cheeks, hearing the sound of waves crashing on the rocks, and seeing spray being whisped back off the surf, saturates the senses with the raw power of Nature.

Although dozens of chalets, huts and shacks dot the side of the cliffs, they do not spoil the scene. They have been there so long (some from the early 1930s), and are so tightly nestled into the side of cliffs, that they appear at one with the landscape.

When the tide is out, the view along Whitsand Bay is further enhanced by mile after mile of golden sands, punctuated by rocky outcrops and stacks. It was here that I saw my first Celtic sea slug – a little marine mollusc that I have been studying on and off for the last few years.

The parasitic threads of dodder.

I didn't stop at Polhawn Fort, but went out to Rame Head. I was not surprised to find that I had to negotiate ditches on the way – evidence that there was once a promontory fort at Rame.

As I negotiated my way around some scrub, I noticed reddish, alien-looking threads covering the gorse. I had seen these at different locations on the coast; while some patches of gorse were

Celtic sea slug (*Onchidella celtica*)

Celtic sea slugs are intertidal molluscs that live on rocky shores exposed to wave action. They usually go unnoticed by casual observers, because they spend much of their time hiding in crevices. When they do venture out on to the rock surface their small, black, rubbery-looking bodies blend in well with their environment. Even when seen, most people would not give them a second glance because they look drab and uninteresting. Seen close up, however, a Celtic sea slug with its stalked eyes, plough-like feeding palps, and pimpled poison glands, is an intriguing beast.

Its evolutionary history is a bit of a mystery, but it's probably more closely related to land slugs than brightly coloured sub-tidal sea slugs. Like whales, which also have a terrestrial ancestor, *Onchidella celtica* breathes air through lungs. Although it can survive being immersed in water, it functions more efficiently in air.

It is a crevice dweller and, like an octopus, it can squeeze through a hole many times smaller than its normal body size. The slug only comes out of its crevice, by day or night, for a few hours before some low tides to graze on seaweeds and small organisms encrusting the rock surface. By taking refuge in crevices, unlike limpets, it has no need for a hard shell to protect it from the waves. This would appear to make it particularly vulnerable to predation, but it seems to have few enemies – partly because it has a leathery texture and glands that make it taste horrible, and possibly because of its unpredictable feeding behaviour.

Onchidella celtica is a warm-water species occurring from Tenerife and the Mediterranean to the Cornwall-Devon border. In Cornwall it occurs on the south coast from Whitsand to Portwrinkle, with occasional occurrences further down the coast to Portscatho; and on the north coast from Bude down to St Agnes. Curiously, it is completely absent from the shores of East and West Lizard.

free of these blemishes, others appeared to be strangled by masses of them. The threads belong to dodder (*Cuscuta* sp.) – a parasitic plant that totally lacks green pigment.

By the time I reached Rame Head, the sun was out, and the wind had dropped. At the headland, I inspected its small, four-teenth-century mariners' chapel, dedicated to St Michael in 1397, and marvelled at its longevity. Then I took advantage of the splendid views back to Whitsand Bay, and south-west to the Dodman and beyond. Turning away from Rame Head, I headed east to Penlee Point and its Grotto.

*The Grotto at Penlee Point – a former lookout with good views across Plymouth Sound to Wembury Point.**

*Rame Head, and the fourteenth-century mariners' chapel.**

*The ferry shelter at Cawsand.**

From Penlee Point, gathering speed because the end was almost in sight, I made my way along a metalled track through woods to the twin villages of Cawsand and Kingsand. These have now merged into one, but in the nineteenth century Kingsand was part of Devon, while Cawsand was part of Cornwall: an interesting state of affairs that, not surprisingly, led to considerable rivalry. There is much to see in the villages of Cawsand and Kingsand, but apart from admiring the very ornately tiled ferry shelter, and sampling some of the local food, I had little time to explore the narrow, steep streets of these historic places.

A ferry runs from Cawsand to the Mayflower Steps on the Barbican, but I had arranged to meet Cha, my younger sister, at Cremyll. So it was there I headed via the wooded delights of Mount Edgcumbe Country Park.

A view from Mount Edgcumbe Estate across Plymouth Sound to the City.*

Entering Mount Edgcumbe Country Park, I thought the end of my walk was only a matter of minutes away. How wrong could I be? After taking a diversion because of a landslip, I took a wrong turning and had no idea of the best route to Cremyll. Through more luck than judgement, I found myself in a field near Mount Edgcumbe House. The view of Plymouth was magnificent. Although I had not followed the official Coast Path through the Estate, it was an easy walk from the field down to the drive that leads to Cremyll. There I met Cha. My trek around Cornwall was completed.

Cremyll at last! My trek around Cornwall was completed.*

Selected Bibliography

Baring-Gould, S. (1925), *A Book of Cornwall*. 5th edn. Methuen, London.

Barrowman, R.C, Batey, C.E., and Morris, C.D. (2007), *Excavations at Tintagel Castle, Cornwall 1990–1999*. Society of Antiquaries, London.

Bere, R.M. (1982), *The Nature of Cornwall*. Barracuda Books, Buckingham.

Berry, C. (1949), *Cornwall*. Robert Hale, London.

Bristow, C.M. (2004), *Cornwall's Geology and Scenery*. Cornish Hillside Publications, St Austell.

Burton, S.H. (1955), *The Coasts of Cornwall*. Werner Laurie, London.

Carter, P. (2005), *The South West Coast Path: An illustrated history*. Halsgrove, Tiverton.

Chapman, D. (2007), *Wild about Cornwall*. Alison Hodge, Penzance.

Cole, R. (2007), *The Excavation of St Piran's Church, Perranzabuloe*. Cornwall County Council, Truro.

Collins, W. (1851), *Rambles Beyond Railways*. Westaway Books, London.

Folliott-Stokes, A.G. (1912), *The Cornish Coast and Moors*. Greening, London.

Hamilton Jenkin, A.K. (1934), *The Story of Cornwall*. Thomas Nelson, London.

Hawker, O. (2003), *Land's End: Walking the Cornish Coast from St Ives to St Michael's Mount*. Halsgrove, Tiverton.

Kent, M., and Langdon, A. (2007), *Exploring the Camel Estuary*. Alison Hodge, Penzance.

Langdon, A. (1994), *Stone Crosses in Mid Cornwall*. Federation of Old Cornwall Societies, Truro.

Le Messurier, B. (1990), *South West Coast Path Falmouth to Exmouth*. (National Trail Guides 10), Aurum, London.

Lewis, H. (2006), *North Cornwall Geology Guide*. North Cornwall District Council, Wadebridge.

Macadam, J. (1990), *South West Coast Path Falmouth to Exmouth*. (National Trail Guides 9), Aurum, London.

Mason, J.H.N. (1995), *Walk the Cornish Coastal Path*. Bartholomew, Edinburgh.

National Trust, Coast of Cornwall leaflet series. National Trust (Cornwall).

Payton, P. (1996), *Cornwall*. Alexander Associates, Fowey.

Pope, R.T. (2002), *Cornwall and the Isles of Scilly*. Landmark Visitors' Guide, 6th edn. Landmark, Ashbourne.

Rawle, D.R. (1996), *A Prospect of Cornwall*. Lodenek Press, Padstow.

Schofield, E. (2003), *Cornwall Coast Path Padstow to Falmouth*. Trailblazer, Hindhead.

South West Coast Path Association (2007), *The South West Coast Path 2007 Guide*. South West Coast Path Association, Ivybridge.

Tarr, R. (1990), *South West Coast Path Minehead to Padstow*. (National Trail Guides 8), Aurum, London.

Thomas, C. (1993), *Tintagel: Arthur and Archaeology* (English Heritage), Batsford, London.

Turk, S.M. (1971), *Seashore Life in Cornwall*. Bradford Barton, Truro.

Index

Acknowledgements

We would like to give our special thanks to our friends Adrian Langdon and Susie Ray who, in addition to allowing us to use several of their stunning photographs, have encouraged us throughout the project. We would also like to thank the following for specific photographs: Gavin Parsons, for the unusual view of a basking shark; Hamish Mitchell, for his dramatic image of the fourth green at Trevose Golf and Country Club; Terry Dunstan, for his picture of a chough on the Lizard; Dieter Fiege for his fabulous photograph of *Sabellaria*; the Royal Cornwall Museum, for its photograph of the Harlyn Bay lunulae; Blue Reef Aquarium, for allowing us to photograph the mackerel in one of its tanks; the church wardens at Zennor, and Revd Doug Robins, the vicar in charge of St-Antony-in-Roseland, for allowing us to use pictures taken inside the churches; Christopher Laughton for a number of coastal views and the cover photograph. We are also grateful for the help we received from Cornwall Library Service, for obtaining many of the books we used in our research; and the staff of Geevor Tin Mine and Porthcurno Telegraph Museum for guiding us through their establishments. Finally, Mike thanks Colin and Katie Pringle for their hospitaility when in Marazion, and his sisters, Yvonne, Lorraine and Cha, for all their support.

All the maps are © Collins Bartholomew Ltd (2008).